Portfolio Careers

*How to Work for Passion,
Pleasure & Profit!*

Steve Preston
The Career Catalyst®

Printed and bound in Great Britain by
CPI Group (UK) Ltd, Croydon, CR0 4YY

ISBN 978-0-9571292-2-1

Acknowledgements

This book is dedicated in memory to **Don Presland** – Best mate, beer buddy, colleague and true portfolio careerist. You are the *'Ace of Spades'* and your magic lives on!

Getting this book published has been a real team effort. I wish to thank some very special people who have turned my vision into reality to make this book into a great read. You are all shining stars.

Steve Engwell, client now friend and colleague, for your all-round brilliant support. In compiling this book you have demonstrated a remarkable range of skills and talents. Much more than copy-editing and proof-reading but intuitive content editing as well as keeping me on track. Arguably a portfolio career within a portfolio career! I feel privileged to have supported you to win through your career change and help you create your own diverse portfolio career of choice. You are a true star.

Santosh Sagoo, having given me the opportunity to support you to win through your career change it has now been so rewarding to see how you have embraced the portfolio career concept and totally changed your working lifestyle. Your support, feedback, insight and encouragement for this book have been invaluable. You are a real 'Angel'.

Gail Gibson, for your inspiration, support, friendship, and many 'colourful umbrella' collaborations.

Karen Williams, author, book mentor and portfolio careerist, for your encouragement and helping me achieve key breakthroughs with your August Book Challenge and Facebook support group.

Dr Barrie Hopson, for your insightful Foreword and support to bring portfolio careers into a new era.

Ed Peppitt for your continued support, encouragement and project management.

Tuesday A. Lewis for your book cover design, inspiration and creative flair.

To my wonderful wife, Lin, for your love, patience, encouragement, unbending support and being my sounding board and rock (*"you aren't going to torment me again are you?"*), on yet another book project and emotional roller coaster journey.

Finally, to all my clients and contacts who have kindly agreed to be featured in the various case studies and examples. You are all inspirations and absolute living proof of how with the right mindset, belief and positive actions, you can create a portfolio career and working lifestyle based on **Passion, Pleasure** and **Profit!**

Foreword

By Dr Barrie Hopson

I was absolutely delighted when Steve told me that his new book was going to be on portfolio careers, as this is something I'm very passionate about. I wrote *'And What Do You Do? 10 Steps to Creating a Portfolio Career'*[1] with Katie Ledger back in 2008, but since then the world of work has moved on significantly, as has my own portfolio career with many new projects and new passions.[2]

It is always good to get a new perspective on a topic one has lived with and loved for many years. With this book Steve has taken portfolio careers into a new era. Passion is a key element and I love the subtitle that links Passion to Pleasure and Profit. In doing so, Steve has established an important new angle for portfolio careers.

---

[1] 'And What Do You do? 10 Steps To Creating a Portfolio Career'. Dr Barrie Hopson & Katie Ledger, A&C Black, London, 2009

[2] Online learning programme to help people design a retirement that they love, funded by Aviva @ **www.livehappier.co.uk**. In total contrast the next venture was one of ending childhood obesity! See **www.five-a-dale.com**. My current project is using gamification to combat mental health issues in the workplace.

On the subject of Passion, there have been some recent findings highlighted in the *Journal of Happiness Studies*.[3] Although the research was on students, the findings were significant enough to get the authors speculating about a link between their number of passions and their happiness and well-being. The results clearly showed that those with 2 or more passions scored significantly higher on a number of well-being criteria than those with only one. So, for someone often extolling the benefits of a portfolio career this is 'manna from heaven'.

I have, along with many other commentators, written about an end to the job for life paradigm as a universal and respected career pursuit. Steve now brings us up to date with many fascinating new developments and opportunities, such as the 'gig economy' and 'digital nomads'. My parents would simply not recognise any of this and indeed would have thought we were mad!

Although I have total respect for all career patterns, whether employed or self-employed, I am old enough to recall being criticised throughout my life, as someone who lacked 'stickability', dedication, or a sense of direction. My head teacher suggested back in 1961: *"On your tombstone Hopson it will simply say 'He was a dilettante'"*. Having looked it up, this means 'someone who dabbles'. I thought that sounds pretty good to me and it has certainly never held me back in achieving success in my career and life!

The book showcases the variety and diversity of different portfolio careers. There are some great case studies and Steve cleverly splits some of these throughout the book to emphasise his different points. One aspect, on the link between voluntary work and portfolio workers, Steve quite rightly has dedicated a whole section on this topic. His case

---

[3] http://portfoliocareers.net/2016/11/15/having-more-than-one-passion-links-to-greater-happiness/

studies demonstrate just how attractive voluntary work can be. Also, why for many people it is one of the main reasons for deciding on a portfolio career.

Steve also makes the point that increasingly we should be talking about a portfolio lifestyle rather than just portfolio careers. This is not only being evidenced by more and more people aged over 50, but also millennials who aren't going to wait years to achieve such a working lifestyle either. Indeed, likely they will not need to do so as companies are going to have to be much more flexible if they wish to attract talent in the future.

In the last century people grew up with the concept of 3 boxes of life. **School** – where you learned everything you were going to need for the rest of your life; **Work** – a job or jobs which kept you going until you got to the final box – **Retirement**.

Now of course we know that just to live and survive we have to continually **learn** about new things and develop new skills. Research is telling us that this also helps us to live longer and staves off dementia. **Work** is also something that people are starting to continue to do for many more years and many now actually look for work that they love. And then finally **retirement** – a term that increasingly ceases to make sense. However, it now provides an opportunity for combining paid and unpaid work.

Our younger generations are already experimenting with 'retiring' from paid work at different points in their lives. Increasingly those 3 boxes are looking more like an overlapping sponge cake with the 3 ingredients – learning, work and leisure, overlapping throughout the life cycle.

More people are finding it difficult to find a job that utilises their favourite skills and also fits their life values. The over 50s are flocking to start their own businesses and are flirting with the 'gig' economy. I am also suddenly reading articles from all kinds of occupational groups discussing the merits of portfolio careers. Therefore, I am increasingly replacing the term 'Retirement' with 'Portfolio Living'. However, regardless of your age or stage of your career, a portfolio career was and still is a great start to preparing for a portfolio life.

With this book, Steve will give you the inspiration and the practical wherewithal to successfully create your own portfolio career and lifestyle. Consider the case studies and imagine what Steve would be able to write about you and your journey towards working for Passion, Pleasure and Profit, in the years to come.

INTRODUCTION

"As I was sitting on the train heading into London, struggling with the dreadful daily commute, something within me suddenly triggered the thought that there must be a better way to lead my life. Why was I working for other people's visions and goals and not my own?

From that moment onwards, I decided to take back control of my life and, regardless of other people's expectations of me, focus on work that I loved and to do what was right for me".

These powerful words and statements are part of a life changing conversation one of my clients shared after she had 'seen the light' and decided she had to change her working lifestyle.

The late Steve Jobs (1955-2011 – American businessman, inventor, industrial design, co-founder, chairman, and chief executive officer of Apple) made a similarly wise statement: *"Your work is going to fill a large part of your life, and the only way to be truly satisfied is to do what you believe is great work. And the only way to do great work is to love what you do. If you haven't found it yet, keep looking. Don't settle. Your time is limited, so don't waste it living someone else's life."*

The Daily Grind

Maybe you have had the same or similar thoughts as you have been doing your regular commute to work, whether this has been on a train, bus or while stuck in a traffic jam. Do you often wonder why you put yourself through the same hell and misery every morning and evening?

Or, is your grind the result of just going through the same old routine to arrive at the same old office or building every day and getting the same old feelings of unhappiness and lack of fulfilment?

So, why do you continue to put yourself through the same daily routine of frustration and angst when there are so many other options for you to consider, especially an alternative working lifestyle?

Can you imagine what it would be like to regain control of your career and life and look forward to doing work you love? How great would that feel!

Motivation for reading this book

I'm wondering just how many of those statements above resonate with you and what emotions they evoke. I realise some comments may feel uncomfortably true. However, maybe they will stir the energy within you to inspire you to take action and make changes in your life by:

- Realising you can make the rest of your work life the best of your work life

- Being prepared to challenge your thinking about the need to have *'a traditional job'*

- Being open to using your creativity in how you work and view work for the future

- Consider the possibility of turning your interests, passions and talents into potential income streams, rather than focusing on just one option

- Developing a blended working lifestyle that provides variety, freedom, choice, meaning and fulfilment, constantly learning and doing new things

- Feeling excited, curious or intrigued by the very idea of a 'Portfolio Career' and the notion you can work for 'Passion, Pleasure and Profit'

- Fuelling your interest in personal growth, expanding your horizons, and pushing the boundaries to challenge the perceived limits of the type of work you think you can do

- Creating a working lifestyle that allows you to enjoy Mondays as much as Fridays and having the inspiration to make this happen!

Purpose of this book

My main purpose in writing this book is to inspire and challenge your thinking to realise that the world of work has changed, continues to evolve and that you do have **choice**.

Also, if you are excited or curious to find out more about joining the increasing band of people who are changing their working lifestyle to work for Passion, Pleasure and Profit, you will have realised by now this book was written for you, so read on and enjoy. You will find a full explanation of working for Passion, Pleasure and Profit, what I call 'working for the 3 Ps', and definitions of a portfolio career in Chapter 1.

So many ways to achieve what you want

I want to be quite clear from the outset how you can use this book to your benefit. It deliberately isn't an 'A to Z' detailed guide of how to change careers, but as mentioned more to inspire and challenge your thinking. However, if you are looking for such a book, then *Winning Through Career Change* has been described and recognised as "the definitive career change book" would be most beneficial. Although there is some overlap it wasn't my intention to recreate that book. Therefore, if you are at the early stages of considering a career change, or working through your options to find fulfilling work that you love, then reading and studying Winning Through Career Change in tandem with this book will give you powerful leverage in making that successful transition.

The power of people's experiences

This book provides an abundance of amazing real life stories of people who have successfully made changes in the way they work and live. It is a myriad of fascinating and inspirational case studies for you to consider and reflect. This wealth of information has been combined with my memoirs, formal research, learning points and different themes. My approach has been designed to provide invaluable inspiration and insight as well as providing clues to influence your thinking to create a portfolio career of **your choice.**

The book is broken down into very specific themes for each chapter and at no point do I advocate that there is a 'best' or 'definitive' approach to create your own portfolio career. Why? Because, from my wealth of experience and knowledge, I have become well aware there is no one magic recipe that can be applied to suit everybody. Although I have created a highly successful six step process to help people change careers, the very nature of the portfolio career means people are likely to have different entry points and approaches.

Like most people's portfolio careers, this book has evolved considerably from my initial concept. It has certainly been a challenging but fascinating project in the making. I interviewed many amazing people; a mixture of my clients and various contacts from around the globe spanning the UK, USA, Australia, Singapore and India.

There were far too many examples to feature in this book and I am already planning a sequel. I have therefore chosen a key selection, which I consider to be the most interesting and inspirational. They are people who have been on great journeys, made remarkable transitions and transformed their lives to now do work they love and lead the working lifestyle of their **choice.** People of different ages, from different walks of life, different parts of the globe, who have all decided to change what they do <u>to work for Passion, Pleasure and Profit, as you can too.</u>

A flavour of what to expect

To set the scene and whet your appetite, I am going to offer some insight from some truly inspirational people you will meet later, describing what they wanted to see in this book:

i. **Gail Gibson** – Business Performance Coach, colleague, friend and champion of the portfolio lifestyle:
   "I think your book should be about hearing stories of other people and how they have enjoyed their own individual journeys, because no two portfolio career stories are going to be the same. I think when people are reading your book it will give them a clear view of the fact that people have made portfolio careers a success. Also, the inspiration and motivation to realise having a portfolio career is unique and remarkable and can be a wonderful life choice."

ii. **Julian Childs** – Who describes himself as a Careers Expert, LinkedIn Marketer, International Connector, Talent Magnet and Opportunity Catalyst. He is another great champion of the portfolio career, having had a most interesting roller coaster one himself:
   "Encouragement to do it, to explore it. Reassurance that it really does work, it is a viable life choice, career choice and career path. A portfolio career is nowhere near as risky as you perceive it to be until you try it. That in itself

is an interesting revelation I'd like to see emphasised to people. Also taking things a considerable stage further, portfolio careers are likely to be the way of the future for the majority of workers. ***So, the sooner you accept, understand and adapt, the better it will serve you."***

iii. The extraordinary **Chris J Reed**. The only CEO of a NASDAQ quoted company to sport a Mohawk hairstyle: *"To show it's actually pretty easy for people to develop a portfolio career. Not to put it off because, although they might want to start a business, they feel fearful of leaving their current employment. To show examples of what people have done and how they built their portfolios. Show reasons why they have added new business strands but let others go. Also, not just portfolio career successes but what happens when things don't work out."*

iv. The inspirational **Feza Sengul** – Internet Entrepreneur and Success Coach, who openly admits to 'failing his way forward' *"I think your book should really help people to take themselves on a journey to explore their untapped potential, because it's not just the cost of starting a business, it's the cost of not doing it?"*

📖 *Case Study: My Story*

From corporate executive to self-employed freedom!

To help place this book in context for all the case studies, I am going to start with my own story and lead by example. This will be a chance for you to understand why I left the corporate world and what changed my thinking about the world of work. Also, how I encountered the portfolio career concept and how my portfolio career has evolved. You'll then begin to appreciate why I am so passionate about championing the portfolio career and lifestyle and have become a prominent global thought leader on the topic.

The end of an era

I had spent thirty years working in the Travel industry for a range of major travel retailers, airlines and tour operators and had forged a highly successful career in senior management. When my company took the decision to centralise all satellite Head Offices under one huge corporate Head Office, I had a key decision to make.

On the one hand I was being offered the opportunity to take on another senior management role in a new organisational set up and be part of a potentially exciting new era for the company. However, this meant relocating over two hundred miles away from the rest of our family and friends.

On the other hand, I had the option of redundancy and an uncertain future. The benefit of this option was the opportunity to walk away with a good financial package to provide breathing space before I considered my next steps. This was a career defining moment.

What did I do?

There was only ever one choice. *Why? Because, apart from the challenges that relocation would have presented in uprooting my family and disrupting the kids' education and exams, there was one overarching factor.* **Most importantly, I realised… I did not want to feel beholden to any company or employer telling me what job I should be doing, where I should live and work and to dictate my future. I wanted to be in control of my own career and life and become what I now call being 'the architect of your own future'.**

So, it was my choice to opt for redundancy, to consider a career change and 'let go' of my past. You will come to realise by reading this book that we all have **choice**. Sometimes making the right choice for you can be either scary or exciting, possibly even both as it was in my case. Fortunately, my wife was totally supportive and was confident I would make a success of whatever challenges lay ahead.

The travel industry continued to be in a state of flux following my departure. Just as I suspected, the Company underwent further reorganisation and restructures. Intuition is a wonderful thing and it is often wise to follow your gut instinct and not just your heart.

But what to do next?

I really didn't know what I wanted to do next in a job or career, except for a vague notion it would be good to be my own boss. Maybe, like yourself, people you know, many of my clients and people you will meet in this book, I hadn't been happy for some time. I had considered other jobs but came to the conclusion I had pretty much had enough working for others and their visions, which often changed in the blink of an eye. So, I ventured into the unknown career transition maze. This was a massive 'leap of faith' but I was confident some good would come of this. I just needed some inspiration in terms of how to move forward, what I could do next and how to win through.

Little did I know that the resulting journey would have such a profound impact on my life. Although I had some 'outplacement'/career transition support funded by my company, this was highly impersonal and greatly lacking. I was fortunate, though, to be offered the opportunity to attend a business start-up course. However, I noticed for many of my colleagues the 'support' had actually become a demotivator rather than a motivator and a springboard to a new job or career. I felt strongly there must be a better way to support vulnerable people at such a challenging time in their lives. Was there no proven way to navigate the career transition maze and make a breakthrough?

Looking back, such thoughts were probably already forming unconscious ideas and decisions in my mind. You may have also entertained similar 'what if?' thoughts, but perhaps pushed them to the back of your mind as life takes over and you feel these were perhaps just a whim.

My voyage of self-discovery

During my process of self-discovery, I unexpectedly developed new passions for career and personal development, which took my career in a completely different direction. This is often what happens.

I cannot stress enough the importance and value of conducting your own research in shaping your career, as this provided me with a breakthrough opportunity. I discovered a government sponsored programme that supported unemployed executives and professionals back to work. Run by an independent training and development company, I attended career and personal development workshops and had 1:1 support a couple of days a week over a number of weeks.

Although apprehensive, I felt reassured I was not alone, as I quickly learned the importance of support networks. Developing your networks and surrounding yourself with positive, like-minded people allows you to share knowledge, experiences and explore synergies – a common theme throughout this book.

An awakening!

During my course I came across the work of Peter Drucker (1909 -2005 – American management consultant, educator and author). He was considered one of the most widely influential thinkers and writers on the subject of management theory and practice. His writings have predicted many of the major developments of the late twentieth century, including privatisation and decentralisation.

I found his following quote to be so profound that it changed my whole thinking about the world of work: *"Corporations once built to last like pyramids are now more like tents – You can't design your life around a temporary structure".* I suggest you read this quote carefully again and consider what does such wisdom conjure up for you?

Around this same time, I also learned about the amazing work of Charles Handy, CBE (an Irish author and philosopher specialising in organisational behaviour and management). He was the originator of the concept and term 'portfolio worker'. Along with Peter Drucker, he has been rated among the most influential management thinkers of our time.

I was fascinated by his views around the changing world of work and how he challenged conventional thinking around the future of organisations. He also described a very different and remarkable way of working that changed my life in one fell swoop. I thought *"this is fantastic – you don't just have to have a job, there are other choices".*

Without doubt, one of the most enlightening learning points for me was the concept of the 'portfolio career'. The notion you could have a portfolio career to derive income from different skills, talents, attributes, passions and interests was not only revolutionary but downright exciting! I just knew that the portfolio career was going to be my salvation and the way forward for me. How right this has proven to be.

The power of mindset

This links to the important and significant topic of 'mindset'. Most attendees on the course missed a golden opportunity to learn and try something different. *Why?* Because, the thought of changing careers was bad enough but a portfolio career frightened the living daylights out of most of them. But not me. Such 'fixed mindset' can be quite debilitating and sadly people will avoid new challenges and can languish when faced with any difficulties. Conversely, a 'growth mindset' will allow you to be receptive to possibilities, unlock your potential and to thrive, like many examples in this book.

Consider... do you have a fixed mindset or a growth mindset? If you are serious about creating a portfolio career of your choice, you will definitely need to have a growth mindset.

In Chapter 2 we will cover 'conditioning'. While some people stubbornly stayed in their comfort zones and floundered, others like me moved forward and made great progress in changing careers and embracing portfolio careers – as you can too. *The reality is you will never achieve anything worthwhile in your life if you don't push beyond your comfort zone.*

Strange things started to happen!

You will read in Chapter 3 about another Steve who suggests that *"by taking positive action you somehow create a ripple in the universe"*. This is so true and I cannot stress this enough. So, although the training course I attended was good, I could see ways in which it could be improved.

My mind went into overdrive, as I felt so in tune with the career and personal development work. I found new energy and a great sense of excitement, which propelled me forward to embrace new challenges. I had the growing idea I could make a positive contribution and create a potential opportunity by utilising my management and people development skills to mutually benefit the training and development company.

I offered the MD of the company some constructive suggestions to improve the programme. I could see by changing the tone of the content from teaching to adopting a more facilitative and coaching approach, it would make the course much more engaging and interactive. This is a style I believe aids learning, so much so that I have since adopted this for all my workshops and Masterclasses.

Then it all started to fall into place. One step at a time, as if by magic. The ripples began to flow in all directions.

Reignited

The course and the portfolio career concept had ignited my flame and I was ready to take the leap of faith to set up my own business. I had a trading name but was still not clear what that business was going to look like. However, I had set my intent and before I knew it I had landed my first ever consultancy work.

As is often the way, this work came totally out of the blue and from a most unexpected source. I was approached by a contact of mine, who had previously interviewed me for an employed role during my transition. Now, looking back, I feel he had already realised what I was gradually coming around to, i.e. my future was best as my own boss, running my own business and using my knowledge, skills and talents to help others. I remember being in a bit of a spin when he asked me how much I would charge. I hadn't even considered my pricing or fee structure as this was all so new to me.

Whatever I said worked, as he made it clear from the outset it was my help that was needed. From the initial meeting on-site, despite my concerns of having never been an external consultant, I realised I was actually coming from a position of strength. The company valued my independent viewpoint and different perspective on how to take their project forward. I was commissioned for further projects and realised I was actually in a position to increase my fees having proven my worth.

As you will see, especially from Jane in Chapter 5, **if clients really value you for what you contribute, it places you in a commanding position to negotiate and determine the terms of any projects.** This might involve the degree of flexibility you have regarding how and when you work or the level of fees you charge.

The dawn of my Portfolio Career

So this was the start of a new career, one that would allow me to embrace my passion for career and personal development and eventually extend this into multiple facets and income streams. Most importantly I was determined to take positive action to make it happen and never look back. This is yet another common theme in this book.

The next ripple came when the MD of the training company asked me to make a cameo appearance at their next course, to share with the group why I had chosen to set up my own business.

Then the ripples turned into a cascade, as one thing led quickly to another!

As a result of the positive feedback from this first venture, I was invited to run a half day workshop. I then graduated to training a variety of full day workshops. This led to providing 1:1 career advice and guidance support, arguably my first step to becoming a Career Coach. In addition, I took another massive leap of faith by suggesting and volunteering my services (albeit partly paid) to help the consultancy rewrite their career and personal development programme. Moreover, this paid back big time as word got around about my fresh, engaging and facilitative new approach. In no time I became their lead trainer and career coach in four locations, whilst also mentoring new trainers.

With such a growing range of varied learning and development activities to deliver, I found I had created a great momentum and my new 'portfolio career' journey had well and truly begun. What also became apparent was the more passionate I felt about the work I was doing, the more the work came my way. The power of this 'attraction' cannot be underestimated, as I'm sure will come across throughout the book. By being opportunistic and taking positive action I had made things happen. I had become 'the architect of my own future'. With the inspiration from this book, you can become the architect of your own wonderful new future too and how great would that feel?

My business evolution

I set up my business in 2002, focusing on a range of HR, Training, Change Management, Career and Personal Development activities. A common denominator emerged in that most of the work came about as a result of organisational change or the need to develop people, especially managers.

It's amusing when I think back to my first business card. I was naïve and keen to share the passion for my business and how I could help others. I had 12 bullet-points on the back of the card to showcase all the different activities that my business covered. I was immensely proud of this. However, knowing what I now do about business marketing, I realise it wasn't so clever after all. Although I was skilled in all the aspects, people's perception of me, especially those I met for first time, was Steve 'jack of all trades and master of none.'

Of course such a perception is somewhat insulting. Hindsight being that most wonderful of things, *I have learnt it is best to focus your marketing on ideally three strands of activities, even if you have more. Why? Because this is far more credible in most people's eyes.* So, **this is my first 'informal' key learning point and tip for you, for your future reference.**

Likewise, it helps your credibility to gain relevant professional qualifications and also become a member of professional bodies in your chosen fields. To this end, I upskilled and achieved the equivalent of a degree in 'Information, Advice & Guidance'. I have also attained the highest level of membership in the *Association for Coaching* based on my extensive training and hours of coaching experience.

Over the years, my company's business offering has been fine tuned. So, although we cover a range of different activities, it's been refined to focus on the aspects myself and my associate team colleagues enjoy and excel in. **That's exactly what most people do with a portfolio career. It usually evolves so you gravitate to the things that you enjoy the most and you're best at.** It's a continual learning and self-discovery process, as you will come to realise by reading this book.

Today I wear two hats

As Steve Preston The Career Catalyst ®: Leading Career Coach, Internationally acclaimed Author, Speaker and creator of inspirational Career and Personal Development products. This is my personal brand and how you will come to know me in the book. The other: Managing Director of SMP Solutions (Career & People Development) Ltd, my own specialist consultancy.

As a company we have constantly evolved and now focus on three main activities: Career Transition, Performance Improvement and Personal Coaching. Although we offer a number of other services, by focusing on these three main strands, it makes our service offering so much easier for other people to understand. Having rebranded, the feedback I subsequently received showed that my company website was clear, simple and transparent (NB: important you get feedback from a variety of sources).

I'm sure you will gain similar learning from some of the case studies. For me, it's now very easy to explain to people

I meet and on my LinkedIn profile that I have my personal brand, as Steve Preston The Career Catalyst ®, and my company brand as SMP Solutions. In my case both brands complement each other, so this works well for me. However, many portfolio careerists have very differing brands or strands of their brands, which you will see from some of the case studies and examples throughout the book.

Final Thoughts

When I think back to 2002, it would have been inconceivable that I would become MD of my own specialist Career and People Development Consultancy supported by a team of brilliantly talented colleagues. Also, I would have a successful personal brand as Steve Preston The Career Catalyst ®.

I am forever grateful I was bold and made the right choice, to take back control of my career and become the architect of my own future. By doing so, I managed to successfully change careers and develop a portfolio career doing work I love. I have totally changed my working lifestyle and now lead a fulfilling life based on my choices. This approach mirrors the many people you will meet in the book who have also achieved success in changing their working lifestyles. I'm sure you can too.

Even better, as a result of my passion for making a positive difference to the lives of others, I have helped to transform the lives of thousands of people with my career and personal development coaching, masterclasses, online programmes, books and products.

I feel blessed to have coached hundreds of clients to create exciting new portfolio careers and also now lead fulfilling lives by doing work they love. Also, by sharing my knowledge and experience via seminars, webinars, blogs, articles and interviews on radio shows around the globe, has helped position me as a key thought leader of portfolio careers in the 21st century digital age. This has given me the kudos and motivation to now bring together some of my thinking, together with that of others, in an inspirational book to share with you.

Inspiring you to open a new chapter in your life

The chapters within this book focus on themed case studies and you will meet some wonderful people along the way. They demonstrate how you can move from the daily grind to a new state of mind. They also freely provide their strategies for success and act as role models to inspire others to realise that anything is possible when you commit and take action, regardless of your age or background.

Although there is some inevitable crossover between chapters, you will find the case studies are enveloped within a particular 'theme'. This will allow you to understand and appreciate not just their journey in achieving a Portfolio Career, but also how it may relate to your own personal circumstances. *Here is an overview of what you can look forward to:*

> **Chapter 1**. **Working for Passion Pleasure and Profit (The 3 Ps).**
> An introduction to the portfolio career, new thinking and the concept of the 3 Ps
>
> **Chapter 2**. **Re-evaluate – Why do you need a 'traditional job'?**
> The changing world of work, the 'gig economy', technology revolution, changing demographics and impact of people living longer, overcoming conditioning to break free

Chapter 3. Reframe to change your perspective
The importance of 'letting go', changing your thinking/perspective to change your life, discover work-life blend, taking back control of your career and life (The 3 Cs), Portfolio Career myths

Chapter 4. Rediscover
Embarking on a new journey, understanding your values and finding your authentic self, have you forgotten your happy place?

Chapter 5. Redesign
The portfolio lifestyle,' colourful umbrella' concept, downsize your career & upsize your life

Chapter 6. Reinvent
Creating your vision for the future, a fascinating look at why and how different people have reinvented themselves, their businesses and portfolio careers

You will have noticed the prevalence of the 'Re' prefix for the themes listed above. For those academics among you, you will know that the Latin for 'Re' means 'again', 'again and again', 'anew', 'once more', 'back' – this prefix was deliberately chosen to emphasise and highlight 'Repetition'. You are therefore being given the chance to go back to reconsider your working life, to reconnect with your values and reignite your career.

Conclusion
The book finally provides a meaningful conclusion. This section provides a general overview of common themes, key learning points and most importantly the difference that will make the difference in creating your successful portfolio career of choice.

Moving onto Chapter 1, we will now get straight to the heart of the matter and look at portfolio careers in more detail and the concept of working for **Passion, Pleasure** and **Profit** (the 3 Ps).

CHAPTER 1

Working for Passion Pleasure and Profit – The 3 Ps

Joseph Campbell (1904–1987) was a foremost US mythologist, writer and lecturer. He is remembered for some wonderful quotes – here are two in particular:

"Follow your bliss and the universe will open doors for you where there were only walls."

"Passion will move men beyond themselves, beyond their shortcomings, beyond their failures."

As we delve into the first chapter and take a detailed look at the portfolio career, you will be encouraged to follow *your bliss* and be moved by *your passions*. We will explore different possibilities, some key benefits and new thinking. You will also be introduced to the 3 Ps concept as exemplified by a magical case study.

The Portfolio Career

So the scene was set and my portfolio career had started. I remain forever grateful to have discovered the work of business gurus Peter Drucker and Charles Handy and their visionary concepts that foretold future working life. You will have encountered these two influential masters in the introduction, and so perhaps you can begin to understand why their revelations completely changed my thinking. I gained a whole new perspective about the world of work, the ways of working and the potential opportunities and possibilities open to me.

What is a Portfolio Career?

Let's start with a definition. If you search on the internet, you will come across various definitions of a portfolio career. However, I have found few that really answer the question in a way that sits comfortably with me. They either mention having 'multiple jobs', rather than just one job, are just plain vague or veer off into 'HR speak'. So here is my definition which I use all the time, when asked the question:

A portfolio career, in simplistic terms, is about deriving income from a number of different sources.

Moreover, to expand on my definition for the purpose of this book and general clarity:

It's about changing your mindset from having a more conventional job to securing an income by using any combination of activities, interests, skills, talents and passions to create the working lifestyle you want. This is what I call working for Passion, Pleasure and Profit, or the 3 Ps.

Taking things a stage further, a portfolio career doesn't just have to be about deriving income. It can be a mixture of activities that allows you to be recognised and paid for work undertaken, or time given freely, e.g. voluntary work. For many people the portfolio career is very definitely a lifestyle approach. You will see a range of examples showcasing different aspects of portfolio careers and lifestyles from the case studies throughout the book.

One of the beauties of a portfolio career is that its composition can change; it is not absolute. People can develop their portfolio careers in different ways. Some people use it as their modus operandi forever and for others it's a transition strategy, one that allows them to shift from one to thing to another. Again you will see a range of examples that showcase different routes and options as you read through the book.

Eureka moment!

In my early stages of Career Development work, around 2002, I remember running a workshop for a group of professionals going through their own career transitions. It was around the time that new Internet-based companies, commonly referred to as 'dot-coms', began to collapse, creating waves of anxiety and uncertainty in the IT sector. Many well paid IT people, in particular, who thought they were on to a good thing suddenly found themselves out of work. The dawn of reality for many of them was they were likely to be priced out of the market. Also, some of the work they did might not even continue to exist anymore. For the savvy ones it was time to rethink and to consider alternatives. Keen to challenge their thinking about the changing world of work and lack of job security, I enthusiastically shared my new found concept of the portfolio career.

I had just started talking about the some of the merits of the portfolio career and one guy leapt out of his seat. I was startled as I thought he was going to lunge at me. I asked him if he was okay and to this day I can recall the essence of what he said – it was along these lines:

"Steve, I cannot believe what you've just touched on because I've been looking for a way to change and move out of the corporate lifestyle. I also do voluntary work at the moment and I really don't want to give that up. Your concept of a potential combination of employed, self-employed and voluntary work is so appealing to me. I would love to develop something

where I can build a business. I don't know what that is yet or what it looks like, but I'd love to be my own boss. I can still do my voluntary work, maybe one day a week, and I'd actually do pretty much anything just to cover the bills. I'd be quite happy to push trolleys in my local supermarket to gain some income while I concentrate on my real passions and doing what I love".

I was totally taken aback by such an unexpected but hugely rewarding response. This guy had clearly grasped the portfolio career concept super-quick and how powerful was that?

So, what is the make-up of a 'typical' portfolio career?

Most importantly, I will restate that the nature of portfolio careers means there is no 'one size fits all' or best approach. I've met many people over the years whose portfolio careers comprise a variety of different options. Some had a range of part-time jobs and while others combined an employed job with running their own business. So you see in the latter example it is possible to be employed and yet be able to develop a business alongside it. I have found this this to be a very common approach. Many people then take a leap of faith to give up their employed job to focus on successfully developing their own business. Once up and running, things will evolve and they will often add further strands, thus developing a portfolio career of their choice.

Your portfolio could be made up in different ways e.g.:

- Being your own boss and having different strands to your business

- Having multiple businesses focused on different products/services

- A part-time employed job and your own business

- A number of part-time employed jobs doing different kinds of work

- Regular interim or freelance projects alongside other occasional work in different fields

- A full-time employed job and developing your business alongside this

- Any combination of the above or including voluntary work

Some Key Benefits of a Portfolio Career

Having a portfolio career provides many benefits. These will become evident as you read through the book, however, from my experience here are some of the most significant:

- Having a range of different strands in your portfolio gives you more security – the increased options means not placing all your eggs in one basket

- If one of the strands proves unviable due to changing market conditions, or you decide to change your focus, you always have others to fall back on

- It can be a great alternative if you want to achieve more freedom, more variety, more flexibility and potentially more money in your working life

- Having multiple business strands means you have the opportunity to develop and optimise your networks with a greater variety of people

- Having a range of activities provides a greater opportunity for you to constantly learn and develop new skills

- Each piece of work you do adds to your portfolio of skills and experience, which you can use to attract more work

- Above all else, a portfolio career gives you **CHOICE**

A portfolio career provides a golden opportunity to 'future-proof' what you do by reshaping your career to create a robust framework. This will allow you to redesign your career and life in the way you want, by doing a range of work you love. Also, if you are someone who has had many different ideas for future work but couldn't make up your mind which route to go down, a portfolio career is an excellent way of harnessing these. Therefore, for many people the Portfolio Career is an amazing life changing concept, just as it can also be for you too.

New Thinking

I have been a champion and UK thought leader of the portfolio career for many years. I have spoken at numerous events, run many seminars, workshops and Masterclasses, as well as coaching hundreds of people to create successful portfolio careers. Moreover, I have used various different approaches and concepts to showcase what a portfolio career is all about. You will read about the *'colourful umbrella'* concept later in the book. This worked really well for a few years, or so I thought. *Then, having asked for feedback from a mixture of clients and valued connections, I was surprised at the response.* Some people 'got it' and loved it, others thought the context was a little too vague and many just didn't grasp the meaning of the metaphor.

It was therefore time to review and reconsider that concept. To my surprise greater clarity surfaced quite unexpectedly during an interview with one of my clients. I had asked Santosh Sagoo for her feedback on my *'Navigate Your Way to A Brighter Future' Online Career Change and Transition programme*. I was keen to learn how my programme had helped her to re-evaluate her career and why she had chosen the portfolio career route. It was a completely 'live' and unscripted recording and so I had no idea what to expect. Santosh astounded me with her unique perception and value of a portfolio career. Her career to date had involved only employed jobs and she was blissfully unaware of the alternative option. She likened a portfolio career to:

"Going into a sweetshop and rather than buying one type of sweet, how much more exciting was it to go to the

'pick and mix' counter and choose the ones you really wanted!"

In the next breath Santosh talked about how, from having been institutionalised in her previous public sector employed role, *she was now working for Passion, Profit and Pleasure.*

Wow, I loved this! But thinking about her wonderful metaphor, I suggested to Santosh that surely 'profit' should come last in order – she totally agreed. So, how important is it for you to focus on the 'holy trinity' in this order? What if you want to focus on 'profit' first, after all money is what makes the world go round, **or is it?**

Why Passion, Pleasure and Profit?

Having interviewed over 20 portfolio careerists and elicited feedback from many others around the world, I discovered there were consistent themes as to why people chose the portfolio career route. These are real-life case studies, examples of clients and contacts that now have a wide range of interesting and transformational working lifestyles.

Even though a number of the people I interviewed are achieving significant financial rewards from their work, not one person talked about money, profit, or any aspect of financial reward before sharing their main motivation to follow a portfolio route.

The power of Passion

In every case it was absolutely clear the person was first and foremost passionate about what they do and why they do it. Now here's the thing… something really powerful I have learnt throughout my personal development work that will put you in good stead for the rest of your working days and life. *Once you understand your 'why', i.e. your purpose or reason for wanting to do something, this then becomes your key driver and call to action.*

There is also a well-used quote to suggest that *'passions drive pounds or dollars',* although some people might challenge this statement. However, if you work on the premise that 'people buy people', then if you are passionate about what you do, your passion, enthusiasm and energy becomes infectious. Therefore, as a result, people will want to do business with you and buy your products or services. It isn't quite this simple as some of the case studies will highlight, but in essence it is usually very true.

Conversely, in my role as a career coach I have encountered many people over the years that have approached me for guidance in making a career change, often deciding to set up their own businesses. As motivation is so important when starting a business of any kind, I always challenge them with the $64,000 question: *'How passionate are you about your business venture and how much do you really enjoy the type of work you are planning to do?'*

Interestingly, the responses have sometimes been quite remarkable with common themes emerging such as *"this is all I know", "this is what I do", "this is what I am good at"* or *"I don't want to work for someone else anymore".* Stop for a moment to look closely at these responses. What do you notice? None of them actually directly answered my question.

If you have to think about your answer, or your answer is solely focused on the rationale *'this is what I know'* or *'this is what I am good at',* then it is highly unlikely you will have a successful business. Why? **Because, 'people buy people'. So, unless you are really passionate about what you do, your work will seem like a chore and you are highly likely to be radiating negative rather than positive energy to people. Not exactly a recipe for success is it?** Can you now see why your focus should be on the 3 Ps as, Passion, Pleasure <u>then </u>Profit?

Can you learn to become passionate about work you do for Profit?

Many of the case studies and people I interviewed regarding the 3 Ps concept were extremely vocal about the dangers of putting profit as your key driver, before passion and pleasure. **Chris J Reed**, a highly successful businessman and entrepreneur, was particularly outspoken. His take was *'if you focus on profit before your passion this will completely distort your motivation, which could ultimately destroy your business.'* Strong words indeed!

To place 'profit' last in the sequence of the 3 Ps may not sit comfortably for some people's perception, though. I discovered an interesting perspective recently that suggests that even if you don't start with a passion for something, it's possible to eventually become so proficient that you earn well as a result. In which case, it is surmised that you can eventually develop a real passion for such work.

To illustrate this point, an example might be you are aware of a lucrative income stream which you feel would be a good addition to your portfolio to boost your profit. One area that many business owners and entrepreneurs often consider is public speaking. *Why?* Because a high profile and sought after professional public speaker can earn big bucks.

The challenge for many people is they have an innate fear of standing in front of an audience and speaking. Sure, as with any new skill, with the right training, hard work and determination, you could become good at public speaking. However, there is still no guarantee it will eventually become a passion. It could easily just become a means to an end, which clearly won't give you pleasure either.

Instead, what if you were to focus on public speaking as a skill you wish to develop for your personal development, as many people do? Your driver will be very different, probably learning to overcome your fears and building your confidence and self-esteem, rather than profit. If you then become good at public speaking, your perspective is likely to be very different too. Without the financial driver it is far more likely you could become passionate about public speaking, purely from the personal reward you gain. Furthermore, you still have the opportunity to earn from such work. The difference being your passion and the pleasure you gain will be driving the profit which is then in tune with the 3 Ps concept, just as Chris J Reed states.

The initial question for me also defies some fundamental principles. As a business owner or career professional surely you should be true to yourself and your values? We will explore the importance of values and finding your true self in Chapter 4. Moreover, authenticity is recognised as a key leadership trait, something that will set you in good stead for the future. Therefore, if you start a business venture from a position of," *I want to make a success of this, but I hope to develop a passion for what I do*", rather than, "*I have a real passion for this and I will work hard to make it profitable*", then you are not being true to yourself. People are likely to see through this 'veneer' and it may have an adverse effect on your business.

Are there times when it is acceptable to focus on profit first?

Of course, as we all need to make a living, don't we? As you will see in Chapter 2, with Feza's story, sometimes you just have to bite the bullet and make ends meet in any way that works for you, even if it isn't what you really want to do.

When I started my business, having decided career and personal development was going to be the main focus of my business and portfolio career, I needed additional strands, especially while I was still learning my craft and developing my reputation. So, although I was earning reasonable money from activities that I loved, I also continued doing some reward and benefits consultancy. People who knew me from my previous employed life told me I was a real expert in this field. However, I can honestly say this was not work I was passionate about. It served a purpose, paid well and I enjoyed seeing the results of my efforts.

Once I had developed the coaching and training side of my business to a reasonable level and started to gain an excellent reputation as a career coach, trainer and facilitator, I wound back the reward and benefits work completely. I wanted to focus only on the work I really loved doing, which although less lucrative initially, was hugely personally rewarding. Having become a leading career coach, the career and personal development side of my portfolio is now by far the most lucrative part of my business. The following points sum up perfectly this whole section on different aspects of passion:

- You can make good money from doing what you love and following your passions

- There is no guarantee money will follow your passions as a matter of course

- It is fine to supplement your income with business strands to focus on profit, but it isn't sustainable in the long term, as you will see from some of the other case studies in the book

I have also come across many portfolio careerists who had taken on temporary or part-time work to help pay the bills, just while they were developing other strands of their portfolio. Ultimately, as with everything, it all comes back to **choice, your choice**.

How will you define your working lifestyle into the future?

So, taking my points from the previous paragraph, what if you were to say, "*I choose to build a working lifestyle based on what I love to do and what I am good at*"?

By doing so, you give yourself a real opportunity to start a new career path and one that is built on passion, pleasure and profit. The concept of the 3 Ps clearly resonates with many people. *Why?* **Because, by reframing your career in this way, you give yourself an opportunity to step away from the uncertainty of needing to have a 'traditional job'. Instead, reframe (see Chapter 3) the job concept so that it's not about a job or a career necessarily; it's about purpose, creating a working lifestyle and generating income in a way that meets all your lifestyle objectives.**

Let's now look at the 3 Ps and delve into why these are so important and powerful – how these can totally transform your thinking about the world of work and what you do. If we work from the basis that we are all gifted with natural talents that give us joy, then clearly the 3 Ps make absolute sense.

So, here is a simple but poignant example of how you might develop a portfolio career based on those important 3 Ps:

Passion:

Focusing on what attracts, interests and inspires you. These are the magnets in your life, i.e. where you have a compelling interest, enthusiasm or desire for activities and work. This could be combining heart, mind and soul.

Pleasure:

This is the emotional state derived when you undertake fulfilling work that you love and are passionate about. You may also achieve personal pleasure from charity, voluntary or other unpaid 'giving' aspects of your portfolio, which you may be passionate about. More about this later in the book.

Profit:

This is quite simply the financial reward you derive from doing work you love via the different strands of your portfolio. This will vary depending upon the nature of the work you do. However, for many people each strand is likely to attract a different level of fee paying work. **Your ultimate aim, as a minimum, is to be 'earning enough' to provide the working lifestyle you want.**

My portfolio ranges from high fee earning work from coaching executives, to the other end of the spectrum; a few pounds or dollars at a time in royalties from my book sales.

I also give my time for free to speak at Business Libraries, Professional Associations and Executive Job Clubs. This is a way for me to make a contribution and give back to the community. On the other hand, I am also extremely well paid as a keynote motivational speaker at corporate conferences and major career events. **Most importantly, it is my choice as to how I earn a living from my portfolio career; you have a choice too.**

In summary, I'm sure you will agree that my sequencing of the 3 Ps is quite different from the approach others take in placing Profit first, as their main driver. Why? Because I believe that if you focus on Profit first, it is unlikely you will be working for your real Passion and therefore extremely unlikely that you will achieve real Pleasure from your job or career.

Such thinking is beautifully encapsulated by the wonderful words of wisdom from Confucius (551BC – 479 BC Chinese teacher, editor, politician and philosopher) *"Choose a job you love, and you will never have to work a day in your life"*.

From a portfolio career perspective, I would modify this to:

"You have choice. If you love what you do, you will never have to work a day in your life."

So, what are you passionate about that will give you:

(a) The pleasure and joy that you are looking to achieve in your working life?

(b) The financial reward and profit to ensure that you earn enough to achieve the working lifestyle you desire?

Don't worry if you cannot give definite answers to these questions yet; your journey may only just be starting. I'm confident as you read through the book, you will pick up many clues to help you gain more clarity and glean the answers you are seeking.

📖 *Case Study: Don's Story*

Jack of all trades and master of them all

Here is a wonderful and fascinating first case study that focuses on Don Presland, my lifelong best mate and colleague. Sadly, he has now passed on, but his spirit and many great memories still live on. This book is dedicated to him.

Don was your typical one company man who followed a linear career path. Although multi-talented he was never hugely ambitious, preferring to stay in his comfort zone and play it safe. Moreover, he had enjoyed a good career in various aspects of retail Foreign Exchange, business development and training roles but was happy just to settle at middle management level.

Turning a shock redundancy into an opportunity

It was over 20 years ago when Don took the opportunity of a totally unexpected redundancy (lay-off) to take a new career path. As his redundancy was a bolt out of the blue, he was unprepared for what lay ahead and like many people had no idea what he wanted to do next. Does this sound familiar?

Long before I became a career coach, I remember having a few 'creative thinking' sessions with Don at our local pub. Like many people in his situation he was initially experiencing a range of emotions. So, besides putting the world to rights I was keen to help him work through the issues to determine what was important to him in his career and life. My aim was to gain some clarity that would allow him to move forward with renewed confidence. Even then, without realising it, I was clearly destined to be doing career development work.

Often when you start to re-evaluate in this way key themes start to emerge. He definitely didn't want to continue in the corporate world and he felt it was time for a complete change. Don was passionate about gardening. He decided he didn't want to work in an office anymore and wanted to be outdoors if possible. Don also hated commuting into central London and being part of 'the herd'. In fact, his daily commute, the hot and crowded tube trains together with the stress of his job had been making him ill. Much to my surprise Don decided to become his own boss, the architect of his own future and set up a gardening business. Don continued running his gardening business for over 20 years, right up until to a few months before he passed away.

Where to start?

Don had no idea how to start a business, so he researched and attended a business start-up course. Interestingly, the trainer on this course instantly recognised Don's own innate training skills and suggested Don should contact his company to see if they had any vacancies. Therefore, in attending a course primarily to learn about starting his gardening business, Don inadvertently stumbled upon developing a portfolio career by combining gardening and training. He was up and running!

Like most career professionals Don had many great skills and attributes, as I'm sure you do too. He clearly liked the variety and freedom of being self-employed and over time started adding additional strands of work. Fast forward a few years and I was following in his footsteps to develop what I then knew to be a portfolio career. I networked Don into career development work, which I knew he would love and would be really good at. Don like me, became really passionate about supporting people through their own career transitions, running different career workshops, writing CVs and delivering 1:1 career coaching.

A trump card

Don also had another trick up his sleeve... he turned his interest and love of magic into another income stream. It wasn't something he had planned for. However, as a result of cajoling from his *Magic Circle* group members and family and friends, who could see his passion, skills and potential, things soon evolved. Don now had a new and exciting addition to his portfolio career as a professional magician. Having previously named his gardening business 'Ace of Spades', by default he already had a brilliant 'trump card' for his magic work. It was clearly meant to be!

With Don his portfolio career was always about **choice and variety,** never about the money. He also wanted to be in **control** of his lifestyle, so he never worked particularly long hours or did anything to extreme. Don was always in total control of exactly what work he did and who he worked for; he would rarely travel long distances unless it suited him. To preserve his independence, Don even turned down opportunities for well-paid full-time training jobs he had been head hunted for. He was also a bit of a fair weather gardener, so his gardening was generally seasonal. Importantly for Don, the blend of activities in his portfolio enabled him to **earn enough** to be comfortable all year round.

As he got older, Don slowly reduced the more strenuous gardening activities in favour of other aspects of his portfolio; especially the magic. As his magic entertainment shows lasted for about an hour or so, he had the capability and the opportunity to do more. He clearly loved it, as did the people who came to his shows.

So, you can see Don was a great example of someone who embraced the portfolio career and lifestyle. Even more remarkable from my perspective, I never regarded Don as someone running a business of his own. He was simply using the all-important *magic* formula of **focusing on what you are passionate about together with your interests and strengths. By combining these to take positive action and utilising your networks, you'll find the rest will usually fall into place.**

A Magical Day!

A few summers ago, Don had the most remarkable 'magical' day. In the morning he did a couple of gardening jobs for some of his regular clients. In the afternoon he delivered a career transition workshop for my company to a group of unemployed professionals and executives. He went straight from there to run a magic show at a local member's club in the evening.

So in the space of one day he had pretty much covered his entire portfolio and was absolutely buzzing long into the next day! A far cry from the energy draining roles of his former employer. Don was unable to stop talking about his 'magical' day and how he had managed to achieve so much by simply doing work he loved.

Don's story and how he embraced the portfolio career and lifestyle exemplifies how rich opportunities flow when you truly embrace Passion, Pleasure and Profit.

Key Learning Points from Don's story

- A portfolio career is about deriving income from a number of different sources

- Utilise any combination of activities, interests, skills, talents and passions to be successful

- Changing from having a 'traditional job' mindset can start to open up new opportunities

- Be open to creating a working lifestyle and generating income to meet your objectives

- Working for the 3 Ps is a great way forward, but remember to focus on your Passion and what you are good at before thinking Profit

- Don had so many tricks up his sleeve – you can see how he could turn adversity into opportunity by just being flexible and ready to adapt to changing circumstances

- Understanding your 'why' is crucial in your career, your key driver and call to action

- 'People buy people' – start a business of your own if you love what you do and are passionate about it

- Developing and optimising your networks will definitely be a key factor in your success

Final Thoughts

From this early point in the book I trust you can start to imagine, and conjure up, the changes that could unfold in your life once you decide to follow your bliss and embrace the 3 Ps. Allow your mind to run free as you dare to consider that there is a powerful alternative to having a 'traditional job'. It's not magic and there's no sleight of hand. All you need is courage and determination and you will discover that there is an alternative way – one that can provide great freedom, wonderful variety, new learning and, above all, CHOICE.

Are you now ready to enter 'the sweet shop' and marvel upon the wide selection of opportunities this book has to offer? Do you favour 'soft centres' before 'hard centres'? Do you favour 'Passion' before 'Profit'? Will you be like the veritable kid in the candy store as you delight in re-evaluating your perceptions about the world of work in the next chapter?

CHAPTER 2

Re-evaluate – Why do you need a 'traditional job'?

My Mantra

"You spend more waking hours at work than in any other activity. Life is too short, so why be unhappy? Take the 'leap of faith' and do what you love!"

In this chapter we will explore how and why the world of work is changing, the technology revolution, the changing demographics and impact of people living longer, how these all have an impact on the 'traditional job'. Also, how 'conditioning' holds people back but how you can break free to become the architect of your own future and lead the working lifestyle of your choice.

The Changing World of Work

It is unthinkable that anyone could have foreseen the remarkable downward spiral of economic events that happened in the twelve years or so from the end of 2001. Major corporations were still seen as bastions of wealth and stability. However, it all started to change with the Enron scandal and eventual collapse. Enron was one of America's largest corporations and the darling of Wall Street. At Enron's peak its shares were worth almost $91 but by January 2002, they were almost worthless, following bankruptcy.

In only a matter of months later, WorldCom corporation followed in a similar accounting scandal of unbelievable proportions and their eventual collapse. Confidence was shaken. How could these huge corporations have achieved such dramatic heights only to ultimately collapse and have a severe catastrophic impact on the lives of thousands of employees, Wall Street and the global financial markets? Unfortunately, things got even worse. A few years later we saw the spate of major global banking corporations who either failed or were bailed out by their governments. The resulting domino effect caused the global financial crisis and then years of deep recession.

These extreme circumstances directly link to the Peter Drucker quote given in the Introduction. So profound were his words that they changed my thinking about the world of work forever: *"Corporations once built to last like pyramids are now more like tents – You can't design your life around a temporary structure"*. Maybe these organisations were indeed '*more like tents, than pyramids*', after all. In extending this analogy, why would you want to 'design your life around such temporary structures?'

The collapse of these organisations had a devastating knock-on effect with other large corporations and small to medium enterprises (SMEs) in the private sector. It gave rise to constant rounds of restructuring, redundancies (lay-offs), lack of investment and growing uncertainty. Public sector services, government departments in the UK (and US in particular) were not immune and became riddled with debt. It became necessary to reduce services, departments, layers of management and staff by implementing the most savage cutbacks. This has proven to be an ongoing theme, as governments and other public service organisations have followed the private sector with continual rounds of reorganisation; striving to achieve more but invariably with less people. In the process of such dramatic change the 'job for life' was gone forever.

The domino effect has also been felt by the charity/voluntary/3rd sector. Many organisations (including one of my company's best clients) were victims of the savage reductions in their funding and have now either sadly fallen by the wayside or are hanging on by a thread. **Expert fundraisers are, as a result, always in constant demand.**

If you hadn't realised before, I'm sure you can now start to understand why one of my key objectives with the book is to challenge your thinking about the need to have a 'traditional employed job'. Sure you can continue to develop your career in the corporate world but it is getting ever less enticing and ever more challenging, so maybe it is time for you to rethink?

Why do I say this? *Because... the world of work is changing and you can change with it too.* **The 21st century digital age has opened up a whole new world of opportunities. There are now numerous ways for you to earn a living other than by having a 'traditional job'.**

Here is some more background and evidence regarding some of the many key changes.

The 'gig economy'

According to many Futurologists, by 2020 fixed hours employment will have all but disappeared and half of workers in the UK and US will be freelancers. How we work will have drastically changed as the workforce becomes 'consumers' of work space and offices become a temporary location rather than a permanent base.

As at late 2016, the latest figures from the UK Office of National Statistics shows that self-employment has increased by 182,000 over the last year, with 15% of the UK's workforce being self-employed. Self-employment has seen a continued upward trend for the past decade, even during the worst part of the last recession. Figures from PricewaterhouseCoopers (PwC) suggest this trend will only continue at an accelerated pace, with around one third of professionals wanting to take more control of their career, what they do, and perhaps more importantly when they do it.

In the UK for the first time ever, the number of self-employed workers has almost reached the same level as employed public sector workers. This is truly remarkable and who would have predicted this dramatic change a decade ago? Such statistics are making a big statement; don't you think?

The rise in companies using freelance or independent contractors for short-term engagements can be found in nearly every industry ranging from education, hospitality, healthcare, information technology (IT), domestic repairs and professional services. This 'Gig' or 'On Demand' economy is now in full swing, so surely not a fad and will impact employee/employer relationships for years to come. The approach is being shaped by business models like that of Uber and professionals sourcing work using companies like People per Hour (UK), Fiverr, Upwork Community and Task Rabbit. If you're not familiar with these websites, I'm sure you will be surprised by the sheer number and type of projects people post. Moreover, you will also come to realise that people all around the globe are creating income streams and developing strands of their portfolio careers by using these online portals to secure work they are good at and enjoy.

Another innovation is the 'sharing economy'; probably the most well-known commercial example being the Airbnb model. This brings in mutually beneficial income for the company through renting out spare room capacity, whilst providing a useful income stream for the individual property owners.

Changing demographics and the impact of people living longer

If we look at the demographic of society today, people are living for longer because they are in general looking at living a healthier lifestyle. The whole pensions' landscape also changed during the recession, so many people will have to wait longer before they can claim their pensions. This means generations of people who actually need to work for longer for financial reasons, or because they still want to enjoy working, are doing so out of choice. Therefore, longevity and demographics will continue to have a massive impact on the changing world of work.

So, here's the thing… if people are living and working for longer then I'm sure you will agree it makes sense to do work you love that is fulfilling, rather than wishing or wasting away the rest of your working life?

Isn't it ironic that for a couple of decades employers have been gradually whittling down and moving out their high earning mid-lifers. Invariably they have been replaced by younger, lower paid and perceived hungrier new starlets. However, employers now face an interesting new dilemma. People are living and working longer but the average lifespan of a new employee is only a couple of years or so. Clearly the numbers don't add up, do they? Moreover, it is inevitable employers will need to radically rethink their recruitment, retention and people development strategies.

Most work nowadays tends to be project based of some sort. Therefore, if people now want to lead more fulfilling, flexible working lifestyles, employers will likewise need to take a much more flexible approach too. This means embracing the unabated surge in the self-employed/freelance workforce, including portfolio careerists. Such a large potential workforce cannot be ignored. But what about their long serving employees? New challenges lie ahead as employers find ways to fuel the ongoing potential and effectiveness of their more mature employees. Instead of retirement many employees will want to ensure they enjoy the rest of their work life, albeit maybe working less employed hours, but instead having the opportunity to embrace the portfolio career lifestyle.

The technology revolution

There is no denying that technology has revolutionised the way we work, communicate with each other and live our lives. **The 21st century digital age now affords opportunities to earn a living that were never previously possible or even conceivable less than a decade or so ago**. For example, who would have thought that with minimal training, anyone with a reasonable business and IT acumen could trade foreign exchange, manage stocks and shares or buy and sell products over the internet through the likes of eBay or Amazon on any web enabled device?

Digital nomads

Digital or Digi nomads (as they are affectionately called), is now a new and accepted term in the work vocabulary. Modern day technology means it is possible for you to run a business, whether service-based or online, from pretty much anywhere in the world. All you need is access to Wi-Fi and a good internet connection. This is another example of how technology has revolutionised the way you can work, which also lends itself to a whole new way of thinking about your working lifestyle.

You will come across a number of examples throughout the book of people who are living their dream by maximising the opportunity of modern day technology to do work they want, located where they want to be, whilst achieving the lifestyle they want. You can't really argue against this approach can you?

Depending on what you do in the future you may never need to rent an office. The concept of working in traditional offices is rapidly being replaced by the ability to run businesses remotely from the likes of Starbucks, work hubs or other creative spaces. As a result, there is a glut of empty offices, meaning it is now possible to rent serviced office space on a very flexible, low cost basis, even including your broadband connection or Wi-Fi.

The changing work revolution

A revolution in the world of work is happening all around us. It is no longer the domain of the mid-lifers/third agers to be challenging what they are doing, why they're doing this and looking at an alternative working lifestyle. People of all generations are now challenging the need to have a traditional job.

We are experiencing generations of new millennial entrepreneurs who never know what it was like to have a traditional job or who are not even interested in finding out. Yes, times are changing and maybe it is also time for you to change too?

If you have never really thought about it, not only is the world of work changing around us, but the pace of change is rapidly increasing, so don't get left behind. Moreover, the good news for you, is, as a result of all the changes highlighted, there is now even more opportunity for you to become the architect of your own future and take control of your career. Therefore, you can lead the life you want by doing work you love based around your passions, interests, skills and talents, based pretty much anywhere you want in the world. What could be better than this?

To give you a flavour of what is now possible in the world of work, in 21st century digital age, let's start with a good look at Feza Sengul, who has truly embraced many of these changes. Having managed to break free from corporate life, Feza is now proving to be a huge inspiration to many people around the globe. You will glean a huge amount of learning and key nuggets from this great example, regardless of whether you are interested in doing similar work.

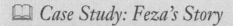 *Case Study: Feza's Story*

The internet entrepreneur creating multiple income streams in multiple currencies, living and loving the laptop lifestyle!

*"Entrepreneurship is the new pension plan
I am no longer exchanging my time for money – it's about leveraging my time.
It is okay to make mistakes in life but don't make the same one twice"*

I met Feza Sengul as a result of being networked to him when he had set up a website to promote personal development events in and around London. This was an ideal site to promote my Career Transition and Portfolio Career seminars and Masterclasses. Also, an excellent way for Feza to leverage his rapidly developing network of contacts who paid to advertise on his site.

Without realising it, Feza was already starting to develop a portfolio career. His journey has since taken him on a remarkable voyage of self-discovery, constantly evolving and developing new areas of expertise and passions. This has provided him with many great experiences, much pleasure and ultimately moving out of debt to now achieving real profit from financial reward.

It was fascinating, humbling and inspiring to interview Feza. I have seen him develop and grow from a shy young man, up to his eyeballs in debt but full of dreams, to an authentic and confident man now truly working for the 3 Ps! Feza is not only living the dream, but he has become an inspiration to thousands of other people around the world to do likewise. Feza is now a true internet entrepreneur, success coach and also living proof that **your background or your past does not have to determine your future.**

Feza's reaction to our interview was remarkable. He was overcome with emotion as he had completely forgotten about some of his major challenges, many of which would have seen most people give up and retreat back into their comfort zone. Not Feza. He is a wonderful example of how, when you break free and work for the 3 Ps, you can transform your career and life.

Likewise, you cannot expect everything to work out as you had planned and Feza is totally open and honest about some of his mistakes and unashamedly admits to *'failing his way forward'*. I love his mindset and how he always takes the learning from such experiences, even more determined to bounce back and make it work next time, whilst **staying true to his values.**

So, meet Feza and read about his inspirational journey. From the interview discussion, discover how he transformed his own career and life and that of many others. He is now truly embracing the laptop lifestyle:

"Everything that could go wrong has gone wrong and most people would have given up by now. I remember hosting one of my first events for my network marketing business. I booked the hotel, paid for the teas and the coffees, set up the laptop and the projector, had the videos raring to go and waited for people to show up. I waited and waited... Then it dawned on me nobody was coming. I had taken a risk and tried to make something happen, but it didn't. This could be very disheartening. Instead, I thought, what can I learn from this experience?

The quality of your life is determined by the quality of the questions you are prepared to ask even of yourself.
So I thought, how can I utilise this opportunity? I've got tea and coffee and access to all this personal development stuff. I really need to learn how to market these events.

So I found a CD and DVD from Success University on sales and marketing. It was like having my own cinema for the evening. I think most people would have quit by that stage, but I believed in Success University, their products and ethos of what they were looking to achieve. So, again I thought what can I learn from this? Although this is a setback this is also a setup for a comeback."

Background

"My family moved from a rural mountain village in eastern Turkey where they lived with the seasons and cared for livestock. They came to London in the early 70's to start a new life in the city. My parents worked very hard to raise 6 children, me being the youngest of 5 boys. Growing up we had a family kebab shop for 12 years and I often say that, 'I used to spice up people's food but today I am spicing up people's lives.'

I really struggled in my final years of high school. I left with bad grades so went to college to retake English and Maths. I also completed GNVQ Business Studies. I was a very quiet boy and lacked self-confidence growing up.

My corporate background was in Business Development and IT Recruitment. However, working as an employee for companies always made me feel like they had ownership of my time and I desired freedom. Little did I know what journey and adventures lay ahead to achieve this goal."

The Turning Point

*"Whilst house-sitting for my boss I found a book on his shelf called 'Rich Dad Poor Dad' by Robert Kiyosaki. This book really captured my imagination as it made me realise that **'profits are better than wages'**. Having read this book, I was inspired to resign upon his return and start life as an entrepreneur!*

For my first venture, I launched an eBay business where I imported USB Memory Sticks from China. I would receive up to 10 orders a day and would then walk to the post office with a bag full of packages. It took me 8 months to sell all of my stock, but I was shocked to find nearly all my profits were gone with eBay fees, PayPal fees, postage and packaging costs. To make things worse, Import Tax then took everything else, so I had nothing left.

*I had learnt my first lesson as an entrepreneur the hard way. In my excitement to start my business and get selling, I had overlooked the basic implications of the running costs. **So, always do thorough research before jumping into new ventures,** even if it seems like a good idea. I just couldn't make enough money, as my profit margins were way too small."*

My new journey into the world of Personal Development

"In 2003 a friend hired me as Business Development Manager for his new training company, dealing with personal development and stress management for the corporate world. He introduced me to the work of Anthony Robbins through his 'Unleash the Power Within' event and I later completed another course to become a Certified Life Coach.

My interest and new-found passion for personal development encouraged me to create my own website to promote a wide range of empowerment events across London. As a result, I started attending loads of exciting and inspirational events, which I would never have previously known about. One of these events was the 'The Mind of an Entrepreneur'. One of the speakers on stage was a multimillionaire from the U.S, Johnny Wimbrey, who introduced me to the industry of Network

Marketing. Little did I know but my life was about to change forever."

Network Marketing

"I was very sceptical about the industry but I was very passionate about personal development. So there was Johnny Wimbrey sharing his remarkable story about how he used to be a drug dealer and he was either going to end up dead or in prison. By chance he met Les Brown, one of the top five motivational speakers in the world. Les took him under his wing and trained him to become a speaker. I was just so moved that I rushed out of my seat at the end to talk to him. I remember saying 'I'm really inspired by you and I want to work with you.' It was meant to be as he was giving another talk right afterwards which turned out to be the very first presentation of Success University in the UK, in October 2006.

Johnny told me 'Feza, your network equals your net-worth.' That didn't really hit me until I started making a living from home because it really was by optimising my network I became successful.

Within two and a half years I had a network of 22,000 people and this led me to do interviews on live television shows, BBC radio and give talks at Universities and Churches.

The business later failed but I continued my journey with other network marketing companies. After more than a decade in the industry I have gained some valuable skills. Whilst the industry has created many millionaires I have discovered 3 major challenges:

- *The profit margins are often small*
- *Not everyone can sell (even with the best training)*
- *Your success is based on the duplication of others."*

My portfolio career today – Creating Multiple Streams of Income in Multiple Currencies

"My portfolio career has constantly evolved. **The most significant component and change has been the focus on creating multiple income streams, but now in multiple currencies.** *This has proven to be a winning strategy because, just as having a portfolio career protects you from reliance in any one type of work, I am protected from reliance on income from just one currency, especially as most network marketing and affiliate marketing companies are usually dollar or euro based.*

So, my portfolio now looks like this:

- *Network Marketing*
- *Property*
- *Shares*
- *Crypto-currency*
- *Top Tier Affiliate Marketing"*

Why Crypto-Currency?

"Well, for the following reasons:

- *It's accessible to everyone*
- *Lower fees*
- *High risk but potentially high reward*
- *A growing trend with more businesses accepting digital currencies"*

Top Tier Affiliate Marketing

"I had a major financial breakthrough when a friend introduced me to Top Tier Affiliate Marketing. I now

work fewer hours but I earn much more thanks to big commissions.

Most people want financial freedom but struggle because they are running around for small profits. I made this mistake for so many years but thanks to top tier affiliate marketing I have learned how to leverage my time and leverage the power of the internet. So, instead of chasing the dream, I am now living the dream.

If you want to create wealth online there are two things you need to build:

- *The first is your **credibility***
- *The second is your **visibility.***"

Property – The landlord

"As a landlord I have an additional passive income every month. I have only got the one flat at the moment, but I am planning to grow my property portfolio because they are appreciating assets and provide a steady income."

Entrepreneurship is the new retirement plan

"You see pensions falling or failing, the age is getting higher and higher before you can claim them and I think people should experience life as an entrepreneur. There are so many opportunities now to tap into, as long as they are legitimate.

I am currently working with many pensioners who need to boost their incomes. The internet has accelerated our ability to communicate and share information. People of all ages and backgrounds are succeeding online.

*Having escaped the rat race and achieved financial freedom in my 30s, I often say that **if you want to retire at 65 that is your business, but if you want to retire younger that is my business.**"*

Share Portfolio

"I am a member of an Angel Club which identifies promising companies that are looking for funding in exchange for equity. I pay a monthly subscription; the club carries out the research and allocations. It is like combining 'Dragon's Den' with crowd-funding. I'm now a shareholder in over 30 different companies and that number is growing every month. So, I have become a mini-dragon."

What does success mean to me?

"Ultimately, success is really about how you think. Napoleon Hill said, 'Think and Grow Rich.' It's all about mindset and how you process information.

The greatest challenge we face in life is with ourselves. Therefore, for me real success is about self-mastery and finding balance in all aspects of our lives: Health, Wealth, Career, Family and Friends, Relationships, Personal Growth and Contribution, Fun and Recreation plus our Physical Environment.

As soon as I paid off my loans and credit cards, I made the best investment of my life by joining the David Lloyd fitness club. I had finally conquered my wealth but it was time to boost my health. My weekly schedule now includes: Swimming, Tai Chi, Yoga, Body Balance and Tennis. It has made a huge difference in my energy levels. Ultimately, your health is your wealth.

Looking back, I remember when I first started out in the network marketing industry when I would drive to meetings in a cheap old banger with a leaking sunroof. I sometimes felt the raindrops on my head and it would make me laugh because I knew I was on the road to financial freedom. I now drive a brand new Audi, which is a real treat and a reminder of the progress I have made. I feel grateful to be living a life on my terms, working for **passion, pleasure** *and* **profit!**

To summarise, here is my key list of success criteria:

- *Attitude of gratitude*

- *Escaped the rat race*

- *Having ownership of time*

- *Location Freedom – flexibility of working from wherever I want*

- *Financial abundance*

- *Leveraging my time*

- *Healthy work-life balance*

- *Investing in assets each month*

- *Inspiring and enriching people's lives*

- *Living the dream, not chasing the dream"*

What have I learnt on my journey?

"One of one of my favourite mentors, the late Jim Rohn, said, **'Formal education will make you a living, but self-education will make you a fortune.'**

So, personal development, for me, will continue. It's all to do with constant growth. I say spend at least half an hour a day developing yourself. It will help you with goal-setting, planning, managing your daily activities and most importantly developing resilience and a positive mindset. These have all been huge factors in terms of my progress and success.

Most people like to play it safe by not taking any chances but I take chances because it's dangerous

to play it safe. I've tried so many different business opportunities. I have failed my way forward. I have failed more times than the average person, but I am not afraid of making mistakes... I just avoid making the same one twice."

If I started my portfolio career all over again, what would I do differently?

"I would certainly undertake more due diligence when first presented with opportunities and take the time to investigate a business before I commit to a contract. For example, I flew out to the US to meet the CEO of a network marketing company. I attended their second annual convention to check the business and to make sure it was viable. After all, if you are going to partner with a company it is important to get it right. This can save you a lot of time, money and your reputation.

One thing I have learnt is to stay clear of hyped up opportunities that sell you the dream. Go with one solid company that is already delivering what it says it delivers, rather than one that is making promises about the future. Focus on what value it is giving today. If it can add value to your life, then you can get excited about sharing it with others and, like me, you can have residual (passive) income coming in every week."

Sometimes things don't work out as you plan them

"There are risks involved in being an entrepreneur. There was a time when my tenants didn't pay the rent. I was owed me more than £10,000 and I just about covered the legal fees to take my case to court. During the same time the traders managing my Forex investments ran off with my money. I never touched Forex again. Although you can make good gains, it is too risky, especially if you leave it to

others to manage your money. Also, the network marketing company I was involved with, a start-up, collapsed.

So, I was hit from all three sides – property, Forex and network marketing. This left me badly in debt. I remember doing car boot sales with my mother every weekend just to put food on the table. I had hit rock bottom.

Back to mindset... **if you look at successful business people or sportsmen you will come to realise: how you react to adversity, the questions you ask yourself, the learning you take, what intention you set and positive action you take will ultimately change things for the better."**

Going back into the corporate world

"In August 2013, I had to eat humble pie and went back into the corporate world as a way to generate immediate cash and pay off my debts. I started working for a business-to-business telemarketing agency in London. It was an established company, representing some major global brands. Going back into the corporate world was scary for me. Having had so much freedom and now having to get up with the alarm clock and commute to work, being on the train crammed with so many people.

I hit the ground running and for four consecutive months, I smashed every campaign. What I realised going back into the corporate world was how much I had grown. This was thanks to all the entrepreneurial activities of being my own boss and the personal development from network marketing. The CEO was impressed and I got promoted to work alongside him. He was quite a difficult, controlling, micromanaging CEO. Not ideal as I like the freedom of doing things my way and tuning into people's needs. My colleagues had bets on me leaving the company in a couple of weeks, because he was such a difficult CEO; but I stuck at it for eight months.

I realised I had so much more potential. If I applied the same amount of effort and time to the network marketing industry as I did in my job, I'd be clearing a six figure income. So I flew out to Las Vegas to check out a brilliant new opportunity, came back and resigned from my corporate job!"

Do I regret going back into the corporate world?

"Sometimes, you need to take a step back to move forward. *I had debts to pay and it was good to take time to reflect. It's given me more confidence and belief that I am on the right path. Going back to the corporate world confirmed that it wasn't for me. I love the freedom of being my own boss.*

*I left the security of a great corporate job to re-embark on my portfolio career adventure. However, that company has since gone into liquidation and laid everybody off. Boy, did I make the right choice to embark and focus on my passion! I just had a gut feeling that it wasn't the right place for me to flourish. **I look back at this experience and realise there is no such thing as job security anymore."***

Would I go back into employment again?

"No way… I am earning much more than any employer has ever paid me. Getting a job now would mean having less time and less money. You don't need a traditional job to make money and that's coming from an ex-recruitment consultant!"

Why would I recommend this type of a working lifestyle?

"Mainly because of the same one word, freedom. The freedom of it and the fun, for me, it's one of the key benefits of having that freedom.

I love travel, go on regular holidays and short breaks and have also had the opportunity to travel to some exotic places with my work. My portfolio career pays for all my expenses, so, true freedom. I am officially a Digi nomad; all I need is internet access. I often make international calls on WhatsApp, Skype and Viber. Technology has really evolved, providing huge new opportunities. You now can be based anywhere in the world, create a global audience and market for your products or services.

Speaking on stages around the world, radio and television shows, being interviewed for books. **It's amazing what you can do when you leverage your time and money.** *Also, it's about the people that you get to meet and* **remember your network equals your net-worth.**

Finally, the best investment you will ever make is in yourself, because the knowledge will always be with you. Therefore, if you want to upgrade your life you must first upgrade your mind. I will leave you with this powerful quote:

"Empty your wallet into your mind and your mind will fill your wallet." – Benjamin Franklin

Key Learning Points from Feza's story

- We all make mistakes and it is okay, but don't make the same one twice!

- There is no job security anymore so be open to exploring other options

- Profits are better than wages – i.e. financial and lifestyle benefits from 'self-employment' rather than employment and dancing to other people's tunes

- It's amazing what you can do when you leverage your time and money

- In network marketing or internet marketing, your network equals your net-worth – you could also argue this adage is true regardless of what you do

- Mindset is everything – especially how you think and react to adversity

- Most people like to play it safe by not taking any chances but you don't achieve anything worthwhile in life unless you move beyond your comfort zone

- Embracing 'entrepreneurship' could be your new pension plan

- Sometimes, you need to take a step back to move forward

- Learn to love personal development and benefit from continued growth and wisdom

- You can now develop multiple income streams in multiple currencies

- Network marketing has made many millionaires **but with 3 key challenges** – profit margins can be small, not everyone can sell, your success is based on the duplication of others

- The importance of due diligence or thorough research before jumping into any new ventures

- The quality of your life is determined by the quality of the questions you ask yourself

- Your background or past need not determine your future – you can take control of it!

Chartered Management Institute Research 2016

Just in case you need some additional ammunition to challenge your thinking about the need to have a traditional employed job, here are some facts and figures from research conducted by The Chartered Management Institute (CMI) in the UK, published in 2016:

'Always on managers' are now working 29 days extra a year and are suffering rising levels of stress according to the 2016 Quality of Working Life study:

- 54% of managers say their working hours have a negative impact on their stress levels

- Working overtime also squeezes out time to exercise and have a social life

- 61% say mobile technology makes it hard to switch off from work

- 54% often check emails outside of working hours

- Managers put in an extra 29 days a year which cancels out their typical holiday entitlement of 28 days

So, in summary, if research has proven managers are working an extra month a year in additional hours, can you imagine how this is impacting on people's everyday working lives? It's not surprising an increasing number of managers are facing burnout each year and the negative impact the 'always on society' has on people's relationships and family life.

I'm sure that such statistics are not unique to the UK, but also prevalent in other countries particularly the USA. Like the UK it's a well-known fact that many workers, not just managers, rarely take their full annual leave entitlement. These facts and figures are extremely concerning. If you are looking to achieve a good working lifestyle, they certainly are not a great recommendation or encouragement for people to move into management.

As you read through this book, you will come to realise you do have viable alternatives to this typical 21st-century employed working lifestyle. *Can you imagine what it would be like to wake up each Monday looking forward to your week ahead, doing work you love and leading a fulfilling working lifestyle?* Great, I'm sure… read on.

I have mentioned the influence Charles Handy had on my thinking. In his excellent book *"The Age of Unreason"* (unbelievable but this was written back in 1989) he challenged convention around the world of work, how we work, how organisations work and need to adapt and change to survive and thrive. I now want to challenge your thinking with two particular issues as they are so relevant to this chapter:

- Why the working week should be typically 40 hours spread over a 5-day week, rather than distributed in the way you choose?

- Why one type of job or career should be considered the norm, rather than multiple careers and switching careers and the way you work, as you get older?

Conditioning

The answer to the above questions, and many other aspects of challenging conventional thinking around work, are a perfect link to exploring 'conditioning.'

What do I mean by 'conditioning'? Essentially this is about your 'limiting beliefs' (i.e. restricted thinking) brought about as a result of a number of factors and influences in your life. Your upbringing, especially what you learn from your parents, friends, family, school, college or university life, conditions us all in terms of our thinking. This is no different in relation to your working life and career. Unless you are the exception to the rule, it is highly likely you will have had, or still do have, the traditional view of the career ladder, i.e. progressing your career over time, moving into management and continuing to achieve more responsible and better paid jobs.

Climbing the career ladder and being able to see that next step clearly, in order to map out your longer team career progression, has been a key motivator for many people regardless of their sector or organisation. Therefore, for many people success is about status and material possessions. Maybe you still feel this way?

However, there is arguably no such thing as a traditional career path anymore, and there are certainly no jobs for life. In the twenty-first century digital age, careers are much more malleable. So what does this mean in relation to your career development?

Imagine the career ladder has now been replaced by the career rollercoaster. What do I mean by this? A typical career path is now likely to have many twists and turns resulting from the introduction of flatter organisational structures and inevitable reorganisations.

Here are some of the thoughts that I had published in The People & Purpose journal:

- **It has become increasingly important to take control, become more like the architect of your own future.** Personal leadership and knowing how to break through the barriers to career progression, or navigate the career transition maze, have now become absolutely paramount.

- **You may have to accept your career might be better moving sideways, or even downwards.** This is a significant shift to looking at careers – no longer as a ladder but as a roller coaster. A sideways or downwards move to acquire new skills, or gain a new perspective, could be beneficial to you in the longer term. This is especially true if you intend to move into a job or career that is more fulfilling, i.e. one that affords better opportunity to become an expert or specialist. You may then grow professionally, but in a different way to a typical line management role.

- **Acquire new knowledge and transferable skills.** Study for a qualification. Grow personally as well as professionally. Positive people who are constantly radiating energy and looking to grow personally, as well as professionally, are a sought after commodity.

- **Deliver solutions not problems.** Problem solvers get promoted, hired for projects or are head-hunted. Make sure you become a problem solver, rather than a problem creator.

- **Build your network.** Within the organisation, think about people who can influence your future. Developing your networks externally is equally important if you are looking to develop your career outside of the organisation. Being well connected is a benefit to the organisation. Nowadays developing a good network, especially via LinkedIn, undoubtedly enhances your professional standing and personal brand.

- **Self-promotion.** Modesty, lack of self-confidence and self-belief, make it very difficult for many people to 'blow their own trumpet'. However, if you don't promote yourself it is unlikely anyone else will do it for you.

- **Find an external perspective and support.** Many organisations provide mentors and coaches. Some companies have formal mentoring programmes that will allow you to be guided by more experienced and knowledgeable senior employees. Professional coaching can also be of great benefit in helping to unlock your true potential, challenge your conditioned thinking or overcome any barriers to success.

Hold on a minute… If this is what is happening in the changing world of work, then what if you change your thinking about the need to have a traditional job?

Can you imagine the opportunities if you changed your conditioned thinking around the need to continually work your way up the career ladder or around the career roller coaster?

What if you changed your mindset from the need to strive to achieve highly and better paid jobs, to that of **earning enough to lead the working lifestyle you aspire to instead?** *How liberating would this be for you?*

Your mindset is key to making a successful transition into a portfolio career. For many people this means changing from a fixed (conditioned) mindset to a growth (or open) mindset. As with Feza, you will see many other examples of case studies where people have transformed their careers and lives as a result of this big shift in mindset.

📖 *Case Study: Tara's Story*

- I want to break free!

This whole aspect of conditioning and how it restricts your thinking around possibilities and opportunities in the world of work is beautifully summed up by **Tara Winona**, a previous client, now great friend and a wonderfully creative and talented internationally exhibited artist.

"Lots of people have nine to five jobs they do for money, and then there are the things that they do at night that might be their deep passion. People approach jobs like they have to be the shirt that is tailor-made for you to fit and, of course, they are not. Sometimes you like to have another pocket, or you want different sleeves and so you want to get that elsewhere"

I first met Tara at a local craft fair. She was selling her 'Reach for Your Dreams' paintings – a series which show a little red headed girl taking leaps of faith and learning to be courageous. She was astounded as I 'got it' straightaway. She was intrigued when I told her I was a Career Coach and spent my life helping people take various leaps of faith. I could see her amazing creative and artistic potential and an instant friendship was formed. I talked about writing a book and Tara doing the illustrations, which she was really excited about. A few years later and Tara had done a remarkable job illustrating my first two books.

Tara already had the start of portfolio career but, like many people, she didn't recognise it as such. She was a creative director and at the beginnings of a career as an artist. Although she was keen to change the focus of her life, her conditioning meant she was racked with fears around her ability to make a living as an artist. How would she make enough money to pay the bills if she just focused on doing what she loved?

Now meet Tara to find out. Her story is truly inspirational. I found it fascinating interviewing Tara, as like Feza, the interview also made her realise how far she had come on her portfolio career and lifestyle journey. She has since continued to achieve even greater success.

Taking the leap of faith

"I have never had what you would call a traditional job. I initially studied graphic design and worked as a freelance designer, chalk board and mural artist; but it never felt right.

Some years later my father died. I suddenly realised that life was finite. It made me question what I was doing, if I was really happy. I decided to close my business and took a sideways step. I became a creative director, travelling around the world for a company performing multi-media spectaculars, using lights, lasers, fireworks and sound. Looking back, this was really the start of my journey and voyage of self-discovery that would eventually lead me to becoming an artist.

I was totally focused and consumed with my shows. I worked on some massive spectaculars, in a very beautiful French way and I was paid to do things of great beauty. 'Son et Lumière', the sound and light shows in France, really are the best in the world and it was an incredible experience. I was paid thousands once to do a 30-second animation of this beautiful laser creation of a car. It was like poetry!

I eventually moved to London from Paris and decided I wanted to get an art studio. It was time for me to explore my creative self. I'd had a rude wakeup call in Paris earlier in the year. I was almost killed by a policeman driving home from work, on the wrong side of the road, who didn't stop at a red light. Months of being unable to walk had left me a lot of time to contemplate. It was time to make changes in how I was living my day-to-day life. Ironically those small steps towards living more fully evolved into big steps and eventually changed my life.

I eventually healed and was back on the road directing shows and spending time in my studio when I could. Then the recession hit; initially it didn't affect our shows. Contracts had been paid in advance and I carried on travelling the world, doing my creative director 'job' as a freelancer and loving it. I was happy in London, in a new relationship, slowly developing my art and life was exciting.

The recession finally caught up with us two years later and several shows were cancelled. Suddenly, I had three solid months with free time. My art called and I needed some time out. I said 'no' to going anywhere else and concentrated on my paints. It was amazing! I looked around and realised wow, I really love being in the world of my studio. Maybe art is possible?

Yet again, I began to deeply question what I was doing. There are very few people who get to direct shows, especially women, so I felt privileged. The shows were my passion. I loved creating them, writing the concepts, the challenge of being on site and painting with light. But somehow it started to feel like it was no longer the only or truest voice of me.

I was getting tired of always being away in hotel rooms, travelling the world. I felt like I had lost control of my life. The phone would ring and I would be away for two months to Africa, Dubai or China. I felt tired of 'the rock and roll lifestyle'. I wanted to watch the flowers grow that I planted in my garden. One year we planted 100 daffodil bulbs but I wasn't around to see them flower until 3 years later! That's what got me really thinking about becoming a more serious artist. So, I began to follow my star."

Letting go of an 'income river'

"I was making good money from being a creative director and life was quite comfortable. I have a very different concept of money now. I spend very differently in my personal life. So, I don't buy a lot of new clothes, I'm super careful. Money is less important, creating art is a priority.

It's incredibly personally rewarding, which is much more important to the essence of me. When I started seriously saying 'no' to shows, I sat myself down and asked myself a few big questions about what is important. I don't want to starve – but if I can create my art, have a simple life, live in a simple cottage and have trees around me, then that's great. If I can be an artist and a writer, and **choose to take on** a few creative director projects, then that's absolutely brilliant. So, to move forward with my career, as an artist, I didn't just let go of an income stream, I let go of an 'income river!'

In the beginning my studio time was an outlet for my creative expression; somewhere I could create art that wasn't dependant on a client's needs or the performance of a show. And without an audience of 1000s. At the time I was also writing kids' books. I'd started writing about seven, almost finished one. So there was all this brewing in my head.

Fast-forward again, I shuffled and gradually wound back the creative director work more, creating chunks of time between shows. This gave me the opportunity to focus much more on my art. I began to take risks and invest in art fairs. My paintings sold! As a result, I got noticed by galleries who took on my work. I started to think 'This really is possible'. A wonderful fulfilling love affair was rekindled."

And today...

"Now I am featured in several galleries, I have had a solo exhibition in London and my work is sold in Australia. Pinch me! I feel so incredibly lucky.

I feel my art and my writing are where my future potential lies. They hold limitless possibilities. I am creating my own projects, my own future. It's wonderful and I love it!"

What would I do differently, if I had my time over again?

"I would have liked to have started painting earlier, had a studio sooner. It took time to relearn my forgotten skills. I got my studio in my late 30s. Before I began working on the multi-media shows I was always drawing and creating, but in a very different forum.

I wish that I had kept up with my own art through those years. At the same time, the fulfilment and experiences I gained from shows has been incredible. When in the midst of a production there is little room for anything else. It's all consuming, so that's probably unrealistic wishful thinking. The insights I gained help my art now and have given me resilience. Being an artist is a solitary existence. However, having spent so many years travelling the world with so many people around me, I do not feel alone in my studio now. I have the world inside me. Things happen for a reason, so it all makes sense in the end."

Giving back

"It is a great joy to me that my art can make a difference. I donate prints or artwork to raise money for charities. It's an incredible feeling. So empowering! I was recently involved in a huge celebrity art exhibition in London, raising funds for the Heart Cells Foundation. Both of my paintings sold and raised important funds for the charity. I feel so proud. It's important to me that I can use the success from my art as a way for me to give back."

What does success mean for me?

"For me, it's about being able to create the things that stir me deeply and express them as paintings or as words – and still being able to eat. That's massive for me; that's success. Having a portfolio career, with lots of different creative avenues has allowed me to fulfil my potential.

Huge success would be showing my work in galleries around the world, having my books published. Also, going to schools, talking to kids and inspiring them, having great friends and family around, living in a home that is inspiring and having a bit more sunshine.

Being the architect of my own destiny. I'm not afraid of losing my job because I have lots of 'jobs' and I am the force creating them. I don't dread Mondays; Monday is just as exciting as every other day of the week. I just love what I am doing – self-determination, self-realisation, self-expression, limitless possibilities and realising my potential.

Freedom, it's great but it can also be terrifying. For me to contemplate 'I'm just going to do my thing, be responsible for myself, generate my income'. Wow, that's terrific! Once I took the leap of faith it was just so liberating and I couldn't imagine doing anything else.

I meet lots of people in my everyday life and they often say things like 'I used to paint, write, horse-ride but I don't anymore'. They look heavy with life. I don't think life has to be like that. I think there are other options. I feel very privileged and grateful that I grab my joy, that I have taken those steps and risks to lead me here. It's thinking outside the box."

What have I learned as a result of my journey?

It has taken me a long time to realise I was being held back by my own limiting beliefs. I used to think maybe I was weird and wondered if I should do what everyone else does.

Thankfully, attending Steve's Portfolio Careers Masterclass helped changed my perspective. It's putting out there the possibility that a portfolio career can exist and that's so powerful. It gives a lot of people courage. It's that old saying, 'if you give a man a fish, you feed him for a day, if you teach a man to fish he feeds himself for life'. That's what I think giving people the concept of a portfolio career does. It's really empowering.

The world is changing so much – it feels to me that relying on one job as security is no longer relevant. I am happiest creating my own future and funnily it feels safer. One of my missions in life is to reach my potential, the highest potential I can, and to see other people reach their own unique potential – what I am doing now is allowing me to reach towards this."

Living the dream – Art, celebrating a love affair with nature. Creating connections...

"I seek to evoke the spirit of nature, give her a voice through the eyes and feeling of my animals; to tell the story of being alive and my own journey through life.

These are things that I cannot always put into words. I want to create affinity with my art, to speak to the heart. As I travel the planet I see people increasingly living in glass and concrete towers, far removed from the environment and each other."

Tara and her husband are now really living the dream and have achieved the enviable working lifestyle of their choice… sharing their time living and working between Sydney and London. They have in effect become portfolio career Digi nomads.

Key Learning Points from Tara's story

- If you keep questioning your working lifestyle and your "*why*" something must be wrong!

- Conditioning is deep rooted and can hold you back from achieving your true potential

- You have to 'let go' and face your fears before you can move forward

- Embrace professional help to help you make your breakthrough

- To break free you sometimes have to take the leap of faith and 'just do it'

- To lead a fulfilling life follow your heart and turn your real passions into your main income

- If you need to keep a lucrative income stream going during your transition then do so, but aim to achieve this on your terms to free up time for your real passions

- Focus on what you want… not what you fear

- Once you start to achieve success you may also enjoy being able to give back

- You can achieve the working lifestyle you desire in most places by becoming a 'Digi nomad'

Final Thoughts

The world of work is changing fast. Now is the time to 'Re-evaluate' and to challenge any conditioned thinking about the need for a 'traditional employed job'. I trust you have been inspired by Tara and Feza's stories and how they have both faced and overcome many challenges along the way. Their stories demonstrate that a portfolio career is not just a great alternative working lifestyle, but they also clearly illustrate the benefits of working for the 3 Ps. You can now see that with the right mindset, belief and positive actions, pretty much anything is possible. As you begin to ponder this now... you may well be questioning the need to have a traditional job.

Wouldn't it be great if you could also make a living from a portfolio career and create a working lifestyle of your choice by doing what you love? If so, consider... **What is stopping you from breaking free and changing the way you work and earn?**

In Chapter 3 we will showcase more fascinating case studies and look in greater depth at strategies and examples of how by reframing you can change your thinking to take control of your career and life.

CHAPTER 3

Reframe to change your perspective

"In the end, it's not the years in your life that count; it's the life in your years."

Abraham Lincoln
(1809-1865 – Former US President)

In this chapter we will explore why **fulfilment** is so important in today's working lifestyle. To achieve fulfilment for most people requires changing your thinking. We will uncover some of the obstacles that prevent fulfilment and explore different techniques to help you think differently to overcome them. By changing your thinking you can change your life, hence the need to 'reframe'. We will also examine why thinking more of a work-lifestyle 'blend' can work much better than focusing on having a 'balance'. In Chapter 1 we had a good look at the '3 Ps', now we will look at the '3 Cs', a concept that will allow you to take back control of your career and life. We will also reveal and dispel many portfolio career myths.

What do I mean by reframe?

The Oxford Dictionary defines 'reframe' as "Frame or express (words, a concept or plan) differently." Why do I love the term 'reframe'? Because it expresses exactly what you need to do when looking to switch your mindset from a traditional job to creating a portfolio career.

As we have seen previously with Tara, the biggest barrier to developing a portfolio career and what holds most people back is ourselves. So, in terms of your own career, reframing means looking at your current situation and what you would like to achieve from a different perspective. It is like the picture you have hanging on your wall that somehow doesn't seem quite right, so by changing the frame you achieve a different look and result. Remember you always have a **choice.**

Changing your perspective (your lens to the world) means working on your thoughts and beliefs. However, this isn't easy, which is why many people enlist the help of a coach to focus on turning negative thinking into positives. When I'm challenging people's thinking about changing careers or their perceived inability to develop a portfolio career, I will often simply *change the context*. I often hear fearful statements like *"What if I can't earn enough?" and I would reply, "But what if you can earn enough? How good would that be?"* This is a simple, yet classic reframe.

Once people have established how much they actually need to earn, as opposed to current earnings or perceived earnings, a *contextual reframe* can be very liberating. Therefore, you can see that for every negative thought there is always the option to positively reframe. I'm not claiming that this is easy by any means, but with regular practice it can become habit and you can achieve the most amazing results.

On my office wall, in pride of place, I have an inspirational picture inscribed with a series of words beneath the heading *'PERSPECTIVE'*. The image features many green fields, some with crop circles, and they extend for as far as the eye can see. The impactful words read:

- Step back

- Imagine the possibilities

- Create the plan

- Enjoy the process

- Relish the outcome

This picture is a constant reminder to me about life being full of opportunity, possibilities and choice. *Change your frame of reference, change your thinking and you change your life.*

To change... you must first change

My many years as a career coach, helping people to achieve successful career changes and transitions, has consistently proven that 'letting go' is the start point to making any successful change. People often ask me "what do you mean by 'letting go' and what would I need to let go of?" This great quote from Deepak Chopra sums it up perfectly for me:

"In the process of letting go you will lose many things from the past, but you will find yourself."

'Letting go' is a big topic, which is why I devote a whole chapter to this in my *Winning Through Career Change* book. If you are struggling with the portfolio career concept, or being able to create the right mindset to break free from your current situation, this book together with my innovative breakthrough *'Navigate Your Way to A Brighter Future' Online Career Change and Transition Programme* are perfect guides for you. Both these resources provide a range of practical advice and exercises to help you reframe in order to 'let go' and look forward. Meantime, here are some of the key nuggets to help your understanding of this important topic.

Essentially, to 'let go and look forward' you must reframe and change your perspective, just as Tara did. In doing so you will open up your thinking and begin to see new opportunities. You are then in a good position to take the positive action required to develop a portfolio career and make a successful career change. Simple isn't it? If only it was!

The good news is that you can make it easier by creating a tipping point, i.e. one significant thing to start the process and create an incredible chain reaction that will change your life. What is that one thing you need to do? **...Start thinking differently.**

Your Toolkit for Life

In order to reframe and transform your thinking, you need a simple but powerful 'template' or mantra to live your life by. This is wonderfully encapsulated by *'The Simplified Law of Cause and Effect'*, which I have renamed and clarified as your *'Toolkit for Life'*. I have done so as a result of feedback from many clients who have told me, that in their view, this is exactly what it is and how it has helped them let go and fly! This is your first key tool to help you on your journey to creating a portfolio career of <u>your choice</u>. Please do not underestimate the power of this mantra *'Toolkit for Life'*.

When we change our	**THINKING** we change our	**BELIEFS**
When we change our	**BELIEFS** we change our	**EXPECTATIONS**
When we change our	**EXPECTATIONS** we change our	**ATTITUDES**
When we change our	**ATTITUDES** we change our	**FEELINGS**
When we change our	**FEELINGS** we change our	**BEHAVIOUR**
When we change our	**BEHAVIOUR** we change our	**RESULTS**
When we change our	**RESULTS** we change our	**LIFE**

Why is it so powerful? Because... in essence, for every cause, there is an effect and by changing the cause, you change the effect or outcome. This simple 'law' is universal and works time and again. Follow this 'mantra', reframe to change your thinking and you will ultimately achieve your desired career and working lifestyle goals.

For the purposes of this book I would like you to consider:

What are you looking to change about your working lifestyle or career and why?

The 'job for life' has gone forever. Current research suggests that most people will not only change their jobs multiple times, but will also change their careers multiple times too. There has been a massive shift away from people seeing their job as a means to end, to looking for a job or career that provides meaning and fulfilment. Does this ring true with you too?

Below are some typical examples that people have told me they want to change. These usually come to light when I am running my Portfolio Careers seminars, Masterclasses or coaching clients looking to develop their own portfolio careers. Because you have been attracted to this book, please consider these statements and see just how many resonate with you too.

You want to:

- Achieve more freedom and flexibility in the work you do

- Take back control of your career and life

- Look forward to working each day

- Fulfil your true potential/purpose

- Find work/a career that is fulfilling

- Start your own business/ be your own boss

- Redress your work-life balance

- Spend more time with family and friends

I believe much of what people are looking to achieve nowadays is encapsulated by the wonderfully insightful quote and reframe from Abraham Lincoln given at the start of this chapter.

This really resonates with me, as so many clients and people I know tell me *'they want to get their life back'*. This is a shocking indictment of the effect the 21st century workplace is having on people. Such statements are also borne out by the Chartered Management Institute (CMI) research as highlighted in Chapter 2. Therefore, what if you reframed your thinking about work-life balance and instead started to think about achieving your desired working lifestyle **blend?**

What's your Favourite Blend?

How many times have you heard the cliché 'work-life balance'? It seems that all manner of professionals use this term to describe what you can aspire to achieve in your life. However, in today's fast-paced world do people ever truly reach that goal of balancing work and lifestyle? I somehow doubt it.

Do you struggle with the vision of what that 'balance' actually means?

When you picture a set of scales what do you see – balance or imbalance? As soon as you add the slightest weight to one side of the scales you upset the balance. One side will weigh down the other. In your mind, as you strive to bring about balance in your work and life, do your scales almost immediately appear outweighed on one side? For most people, this is the case.

Does the word 'balance' set the highest benchmark as being a state of perfection?

We all know that even with the best will and intention, achieving a perfect work-life balance is unlikely. Life happens. Work happens. Challenges, diversions and situations take place. That's the real world. Are you expecting too much of yourself if you aim for the perfect balance? In other words, are you setting yourself an unrealistic and unattainable goal? The reality is very few people will ever achieve a truly balanced working lifestyle and, in any event, many people don't necessarily want this anyway.

I'm sure we all know people whose ideal working lifestyle is balanced more in favour of 'work' than 'life'. I once worked with a client who had a reasonably successful business but was looking to diversify and develop a portfolio career. He proudly boasted he *'didn't do holidays'*. My previous working background in the travel industry meant that such a statement was quite alien to me. Life would be very boring if we all did and felt the same about everything, wouldn't it? I wondered how his wife felt about this as I know people can be quite ambivalent about holidays, which can cause friction in relationships. He later told me his wife went on holidays with her friends while he stayed home and ran his business. **Wouldn't you prefer to bring about a better sense of unity in your work and life?**

In such circumstances it may be better to simply **'blend'** what you do. Let's consider the word 'blend'. To **blend** evokes a new meaning; one where you can <u>mix</u> your work and lifestyle together. Blending can soften the idea of having to achieve that perfect balance, don't you think? Blending negates the need for a defined edge or boundary and instead it suggests the opportunity to merge or combine. As my client was looking to rethink his business, I felt that by taking time out for a holiday would have helped him reframe and gain a new perspective. He clearly felt his chosen blend was 80% work and 20% life. This was his choice and it seemed to work well for him and his wife in their personal circumstances.

Does blending encourage you to change your perspective about how your work and lifestyle can complement one another?

Together with living in a fast-paced world, the changing world of work is moving at a rapid pace as well. With growing numbers of people embracing portfolio careers and lifestyles, the concept of blending is becoming more and more apparent. A portfolio approach allows you to create a working lifestyle which clearly resonates with the term 'blending'. A working lifestyle is a **blend** of work and living, where you can combine what you do with how you choose to live your life. **Blend** says 'together', 'combination' and 'many separates become one'.

So why blend?

To conclude, balance is often subjective and we all view it differently. For some it can be weighted in favour of 'work time' and for others 'leisure time'. Consequently, work-life balance isn't necessarily *evenly* balanced. In many ways it is just like our varied tastes in coffee – you can find the right blend for you to give you the satisfaction you desire.

So, throw away the scales in your work and life. Reframe and change your perspective from balance to **blend**. Set yourself a new challenge… to discover your favourite **blend** of work and lifestyle. You will certainly find this reframe a great help when looking to create your portfolio career of choice.

Taking back Control of your Career and Life – The 3 Cs

I'm sure you have now understood and bought into the concept of working for the 3 Ps. Let's now look at the concept of the 3 Cs. These three words and are also extremely powerful. They are integral to getting the right blend for you and key to having a successful portfolio career:

- CHOICE

- CONTROL

- CLARITY

Unless you have studied for a particular profession, e.g. Doctor or Lawyer, most people fall into their jobs or careers by accident rather than by design. Once this process begins many people continue doing the same or similar work, often in the same working sector, for many years to come. This perpetuates until circumstances abruptly change, or you have a sudden realisation that can be linked to any of the following:

- Becoming stuck in a rut, unfulfilled, going nowhere

- Not achieving or aware of your true potential

- Suffering a job loss as a result of redundancy/lay offs

- Returning to work after a career break and wanting something very different

- Desire to find more fulfilling and enjoyable work

- Reaching a career crossroads in your life and unsure how to move forward

- There becomes a need to make a **choice** about the future

From choice comes **freedom**. You can choose what work you do, how you work, when you work, when you take your holidays, what type of clients or customers you want and how much you charge for your products or services. This list goes on.

The choices you make will help you take back control of your career and life. As I started to write this section, I heard from a most frustrated client. Given only a few days' notice, he was told he must change his work shift patterns for the next few weeks and therefore needed to reschedule his coaching session with me. He was concerned for the delays as a result of this imposition, but unfortunately had no option. One of his main reasons for seeking a career change was to break free and regain control over his life.

Likewise, I'm sure we all know people who are only allowed to take their holidays when it suits their employer. Often seniority dictates who gets first option with annual leave arrangements. Invariably there will be other factors, such as ensuring sufficient number of staff are present to cover service delivery. The latter is perhaps more reasonable but wouldn't it be liberating for you to be able to exercise your own choice?

Having **choice** and taking back **control**, help to give you the **clarity** that is needed to create a successful portfolio career. Clarity in terms of doing what is right for you to create the working lifestyle you want.

So, instead of having a 'traditional job' how would it be to:

- Make the rest of your work life, the best of your work life?

- Explore new ways of working and earning a living?

- Change your thinking about what work you can do?

- Derive income from different interest, skills, talents and passions?

As you think about your career it is a good idea to look at the path you are currently travelling. Is your path similar to the well-used ski run? Have you taken a 'traditional' or 'safe' route, just as we saw with Don's case study in Chapter 1? As you travel along your journey, have you ever stepped out of your comfort zone and chosen another way?

I have already challenged the career ladder. Also, a typical linear career path is just like it says. It's a straight line, with no bumps or diversions. In many cases your path may have begun with the choices you made in the subjects you studied at school, college or university. Next you entered the world of work, maybe falling into a job or career, then establishing a definite career direction as your main focus. As you have worked and developed your career over the years, you are likely to have remained true to this linear path. *But has your linear path remained true to who you are? Are you happy and fulfilled in your career?*

As we are now challenging convention, let's now challenge some typical conditioned thinking around portfolio careers. Such thinking can hold back many people from even starting down the road of a portfolio career, but you won't let this happen to you, will you?

Ten Portfolio Career Myths

There are numerous myths about portfolio careers, which you may have also come across. Some of these myths may even be the reason why you have not taken the 'leap of faith' to create your own portfolio career. I am now going to focus on the top ten myths I have discovered throughout my extensive coaching career. I call these 'myths' as I have learned that they are no more than perceptions; a distorted reality that can be changed by reframing your thinking.

Myth One – Portfolio careers are only for creative people e.g. musicians, artists, writers etc.

Reality – Many creative people are attracted to the variety, freedom and working lifestyle of a portfolio career, just as we have seen from Tara back in Chapter 2. However, reality for many creative people is that it can be extremely difficult to make a living from one passion or income stream. Naturally this doesn't apply to just creative people as you will see in a number of examples throughout the book.

Throughout the world of music there is an abundance of great musicians who struggle to make a living doing what they love. In order to survive, many supplement their passion with additional income streams. **Michelle Urquhart** is a great example.

She lives in Sydney, Australia and is a highly trained, talented and experienced classical violist and violinist. By the nature of her work she is 'freelance'. When I interviewed her she had recently returned from a successful solo recital tour of Italy, with her pianist. Such lucrative opportunities are few and far between. To earn a decent living and have the working lifestyle Michelle desires, she needs to supplement her income with other activities. As well as playing, she also teaches music privately. Not only does this bring in useful income, such work can also be managed flexibly, around her concerts and personal practice time. Michelle's love of music flows through her teaching and performing. She is especially passionate about Chamber Music.

Most interestingly though, Michelle has another, somewhat unusual strand to her portfolio… she works one day a week at a local pharmacy. *Why?* Because, she says it is great to be helping in the local community and she enjoys having 'real' human contact. In the world of music, she is constantly meeting musicians, who are very definitely of a different mindset and ilk. Working in the shop also helps to get her known in the community for her music. Her customers help to spread the word about her concerts, which is a great way of developing advocates for her music and they are also doing the marketing for her!

Marc Bake-Will is a comedy writer with great experience in writing for various formats from gags to episode length narrative. He is also a triathlete. This clearly requires much time training, but this has become a key part of his 'blended' portfolio working lifestyle.

Although Marc has achieved a reasonable level of success with his creative writing with comedy shows commissioned for TV and plays that have made theatre. As with Tara and Michelle, his is a highly competitive market. It is really tough to achieve that big breakthrough, especially to get regular commissions to write top comedy shows for TV. Apart from a few years when Marc taught English as a foreign language while working in Europe, he has never had a 'traditional job'.

"I came back to England and thought, 'What do I want to do?' I knew I didn't want to have a traditional career. I've got friends who are accountants, lawyers, headmasters, and I've seen the sacrifices they've had to make in their personal life in order to thrive. I thought, I don't want to do that. So I set out to be a comedy writer but you can't expect to earn money from your writing straight away. Therefore, you need another source of income.

Through my first comedy writing partner, I met the MD of a small but growing business who was looking for some admin help. The two things dovetailed perfectly because I now had another income stream to help tide me over while I was developing my comedy writing skills. Things have evolved over the years. My role and skills have developed with the business. I'm now doing much more advanced admin work, IT and financial reporting. My writing career has also developed at the same time. It wasn't a plan, it just happened like that. It's great because it works for us both, so I've stuck with it."

Marc is a great believer in the power of collaborations and acknowledges his successful comedy writing partnership. He also believes it is important to continue to develop personally and professionally and is not content to rest on his laurels. The value of collaboration and ongoing personal/professional develop are important recurring themes you will see throughout this book. Marc has continued to develop his skills in both the creative writing and business side of his portfolio. He is now a published author of comedy books and also does comedy copywriting for online videos and greetings cards. In addition, Marc is also undertaking formal financial qualifications.

How does Marc feel his different strands have worked to his benefit?

"It has definitely been more by accident than design. However, the longer my portfolio career has developed the more I've

realised both income streams actually influence the other and maximise my skill-set. Therefore, if I took one strand away and just focused on the other full time, I think I would enjoy my work less and I'm also not sure I'd be as effective."

We will revisit Marc in Chapter 5 and consider a most interesting dilemma he highlighted, which will make far more sense in the context of that section of the book.

Myth Two – I'm too young to have a portfolio career

Reality – In the 21st century digital age, if you like the idea of doing different 'stuff', have the courage to try different ways of deriving income, some entrepreneurial spirit, bags of enthusiasm and determination to make it work, then you can never be too young to develop a portfolio career. With such positive attributes, you will also have a great chance of making it work. There are now loads of examples of young people who leave college or university and never have a traditional job. Instead, even though they may not recognise the term portfolio career, they build a business based on a variety of skills, passions, interests and talents. They may even become serial freelancers in different fields of work. Many business gurus believe it will become commonplace for young people to view a portfolio career as an acceptable and viable option to a traditional employed job.

Myth Three – I'm too old to have a portfolio career

Reality – As I have proven many times with my clients and people I know, age is just a smokescreen. Many people either want to work longer, as they are living longer or want to stay active in mind and body, or need to work longer due to their pension situation or other financial reasons. Either way most people want to be able to spend the rest of their working lives doing work they enjoy. Work that provides them with enough income to have the working lifestyle of their choice in the twilight years of their career. I have worked with clients and know of many other people who have gravitated to the portfolio career concept and created their portfolios of choice well into their 60s and even 70s.

Chris King is a champion of the portfolio career in the USA. Remarkably, Chris has enjoyed a portfolio career for well over 25 years. Why 'remarkable'? Because, despite having passed the grand old age of 80, she is still working a full week with a varied portfolio lifestyle. Amusingly, one of her portfolio strands is running keep fit classes for 'oldies'. Ironically, Chris is at least a decade older than any of her class!

Myth Four – Portfolio careers are mainly for women returners, who just want to dabble and have a hobby business

Reality – The portfolio career concept and lifestyle is very appealing to many women who return to work after taking a career break to raise a family. They value the flexibility and variety that can be achieved. However, women returners certainly don't make up the majority of portfolio careerists. Equally, although some women may be happy to just 'dabble with a hobby business', many women returners find their real passions and also develop an entrepreneurial spirit. The difference being they are creating their portfolio of choice, running successful businesses doing work they love, but developing their working lifestyle around their family commitments.

Myth Five – Portfolio careers are only for people who have either been made redundant (laid off) who can't find another job

Reality – it is true that many people who've been laid off will be quite rightly re-evaluating their career options. I heartily encourage people to do this in my internationally acclaimed book *'Winning Through Redundancy'*. Having done much work, supporting people to win through redundancy and change their thinking about what might be possible moving forward, I have found an increasing number of people are attracted to the portfolio career concept. Going down the portfolio career route is a great way for career professionals to rekindle and redesign their careers to do work they love and achieve the working lifestyle they want. As I'm sure you have realised by now, creating a portfolio career is certainly not just the domain of people affected by redundancy or layoffs.

Myth Six – Portfolio careers are only for people who don't want a 'proper job'

Reality – This is an interesting one. *Why?* …Because there is an element of truth in this. I have coached many people over the years and also know many others who no longer want what some people may term as a 'proper job'. This is exactly the concept I was challenging in Chapter 2, i.e. the need to have a traditional employed job. Whilst portfolio careers are absolutely ideal for people with such a mindset, it is nonsense to suggest that portfolio careers are only suitable for this group of people.

Myth Seven – How do you expect me to get multiple jobs with a Portfolio career when I am struggling to get one?

Reality – The answer quite simply is I don't! Interestingly, this is a comment that has often been made at various seminars and workshops I have run over the years. Such comments tend to be made by people who just don't understand the portfolio concept. A portfolio career can be based on having multiple jobs, although this is not commonplace. However, I will share a case study in Chapter 5 of someone whose portfolio career is made up of running multiple businesses as separate limited companies. Many people also have portfolio careers made up of various part-time employed jobs. The difference in both these respects is all about **choice**.

Myth Eight – People who have portfolio careers are 'jack of all trades and master of none'

Reality – This is another common comment or viewpoint. I tend to find it stems from people who either don't really understand the portfolio career concept or, quite often, people who are envious of people with portfolio careers. This might be a typical comment from someone who is bored with what they do and not achieving their true potential. Seeing other people who do have great variety in their work, who are actually good at many things and making it work for them, often rankles with them. The best answer is of course to join the happy portfolio careerists. I will also show you through a mixture of inspirational case studies, other key content and learning points in the book that **you can in fact be 'Jack of many trades and master of many'** ...you only have to look back at Don's case study in Chapter 1.

Myth Nine – You will never make money (or enough money) from your passions

Reality – I definitely agree that some passions will never make you enough money to earn a decent living and cover your costs. But what if you reframe your thinking to one of *"I know this passion/activity will never earn me much, but as I love doing this work it would be great to include this as part of my portfolio of choice… it's just not my main income stream."*

A great example of this strategy was with a client who attended one of my workshops a number of years ago. She was in transition between jobs and struggling to get her head around what to do next. She was an experienced graphic designer but, by her own admission she had fallen out of love with her profession. When we explored her passions and what she enjoyed doing the most, she would come to life when sharing her love and interest in making custom jewellery. Although she loved making custom jewellery and got immense enjoyment and satisfaction from seeing the end result, she felt she couldn't make a living from it as people weren't prepared to pay much for custom jewellery.

You could argue her perception was a classic limiting belief, as I'm sure there are plenty of people who actually do make a living from selling custom jewellery via eBay, Etsy and high profile craft fairs. However, the reality is to do so is all about volume. She could have been spending hours, days, weeks creating jewellery and of course, time is money. Therefore, she was probably right in her thinking.

In a classic reframe, I suggested to her what if she changed her thinking, so creating and selling custom jewellery become part of a portfolio career? This way she could derive income from other skills, talents, interests and passions, to enable her to earn enough but still do what she loves.

Her reaction was instant. She was blissfully unaware of the portfolio career concept, but once I had explained this she began to instantly visualise how she could make this happen. Within minutes she had a lightbulb moment and exclaimed:

"I've got it… I would still be happy to do graphic design but more so on my terms, ideally as a freelancer or maybe even a part-time employed role. I could still create my custom jewellery and develop other passions and interests alongside this. I could probably earn enough from my graphic design work to fund my other passions and interests. That would be great!"

In one magic moment this talented woman had created in her own mind a potential portfolio career of choice.

Myth Ten – By doing what you love, the money will follow

Reality – In Chapter 1 we looked in depth at the 3 Ps and whether 'passions can drive pounds or dollars'. However, like anything in life you need to put in the effort and take the right positive action to gain the benefit. "You reap what you sow", as the saying goes. Therefore, just because you love what you do doesn't mean to say that you will be able to make your portfolio career a financial success. **You also need to love putting in the work to make it happen!**

Catastrophe or Opportunity?

Experience tells me that people of all ages are now embracing the portfolio career concept. Regardless of age there are great opportunities ranging from post college students, who may never have had a 'proper job', to those in their third age who either need to continue to work or just want to continue to work as we are living longer.

What is becoming more prevalent these days is that people, regardless of age, will periodically take stock to review and reconsider their future work plans throughout working life. As work situations and personal circumstances change people realise they may not be able, nor want to continue, to do the same type of work or work in the same way as they have done during their earlier career.

As organisations continue to strive for improved efficiencies and cost savings, their actions invariably result in some form of restructuring or large scale reorganisation. Such imposed change often creates uncertainty and increased stress levels when facing the fear of redundancy. For many this situation may be regarded as a catastrophe, but reframing mindset could provide quite a different outcome.

You may have experienced similar situations in your career, or know other people who have been affected. If so you will know how these circumstances can negatively impact on emotions, behaviour and wellbeing. However, when you decide to take positive action to regain control over your career options, any fears begin to dissipate and new doors begin to open. The following case study is an excellent example of change imposed during the latter part of a lengthy, successful career and how adversity can be reframed as opportunity.

📖 Case Study: Steve's Story (Part 1)

Learning to let go and embrace a portfolio career in his late 50s

Steve Engwell had worked in Human Resources roles in the public sector, local government, for almost 40 years and headed up the Learning and Organisational Development function during his final years. As with many public service organisations around the world, the financial crisis of recent times meant his employer had to change focus and reduce costs by achieving efficiency savings. The absence of any funding for new and exciting projects led him to feel that he wasn't able to use his talents to best ability and began feeling stymied by the circumstances. A major reorganisation was implemented and Steve's senior position was vulnerable; he soon became another casualty of compulsory redundancy.

Now is his late 50s and in need of guidance and direction, Steve investigated the possibility of securing Executive Outplacement/Career Transition coaching to help challenge and reframe his view of the future. I first met Steve when a mutual contact, recommended him to my company. Steve wanted a bespoke, personalised programme of support to help him through this challenging and daunting time. He was fortunate that it was to be something very different to the typical standard approach available to most staff in this position. Like so many public servants hit by the recession, Steve had never experienced job loss before and was now facing an uncertain future.

Now meet Steve for the first part of his inspirational insights into how his portfolio career unfolded and came together, as we explore some of the key extracts from his fascinating interview.

"All I knew was I wanted to continue working, continue to contribute and help others by making a difference in some way. I was fortunate that my pension and benefits package had been released early so I had a financial cushion during my transition. However, the great question remained in my mind... 'what could someone who has spent their entire career in public sector organisations do late in his working life?'

It is often said that things happen for a reason and little did I know that I was about to embark on an incredible voyage of self-discovery that would completely transform my career and life!"

The reframe

"From the outset, my biggest challenge was 'letting go'. My initial reaction to redundancy was 'I need another similar job'. I couldn't see past this, although deep down my instincts were telling me it was time to change. But change to what and how?

I got real benefit from the coaching support from Steve and his colleagues, together with attending a couple of great Masterclasses, as part of my Career Transition programme. One was on changing careers and the other on creating a portfolio career. These were so different to anything I had ever experienced and it really helped me to start to see things from a different perspective.

By learning to reframe, I gradually started to come to terms with my situation and realised maybe this was really a time of opportunity rather than a threat. I became determined to enjoy this new voyage of self-discovery into the unknown. I systematically followed Steve's **Six Step Career Navigation Cycle** *process and my focus changed to one of 'possibility', as I moved from what I called 'chaos towards clarity.'*

My journey and voyage of self-discovery was definitely an emotional roller coaster ride. It certainly wasn't plain sailing. There were many twists, turning points, ups and downs and pivotal moments along the way. Without doubt the biggest and most impactful insight for me was the realisation there were alternatives to having a 'traditional job'. I had certainly never heard of a portfolio career. This was a fantastic revelation which created great intrigue for me. Although such an option seemed way out of my reach, I really enjoyed discovering how I could apply myself to such a very different approach to work and earning a living.

I found the portfolio career option really challenged my thinking. The opportunity to completely rethink my working lifestyle definitely gave me the motivation to let go of my corporate working life and make my change. I really liked the idea of having the flexibility to work when and how I wanted. I wasn't even sure I wanted the stress of working full time again. Steve kept telling me I could become 'the architect of my own future'. As I reframed even more, I got excited at the thought of creating my portfolio career and having choice in the work I considered as I moved forward."

Light bulb moments

"Light bulbs began to flicker in my coaching session with Steve. I remember he was sharing a simple concept of 'comfort zones and stretch zones' and a list of for mindset attributes that related to both. He had sketched a rough drawing, which he had intended to use for a Masterclass. I remember asking if he would like me to tidy it up for him. He was surprised but clearly delighted at my offer. **This was the first dawning of realisation that people appreciated something I had taken for granted, i.e. my IT skills.**

I turned Steve's idea into an impactful PowerPoint slide and he quickly realised I had an excellent grasp and a natural creative flair working with MS PowerPoint and other software. This was the start of creating many other presentations for his seminars, workshops and Masterclasses. I was now getting regular challenges from Steve for his projects that allowed me to put my creative stamp on such great ideas.

My presentations were very different, much more dynamic and visually impactful. Then Steve asked me if I was familiar with something called 'Prezi'?' I wasn't, so I researched it and taught myself how to use Prezi. I found Prezi wasn't particularly difficult to learn or use. However, yet again, Steve pointed out, this wasn't the norm as he had shied away from it. He insisted I must have a natural talent for such software. The reality was I had now found another exciting and dynamic medium for presentations, which not many people had knowledge of how to use effectively! Gradually, the whole IT side started to open up for me, as word got around and I was being asked to create dynamic, impactful presentations for a number of new contacts in an ever growing network."

The power of the metaphor

"Another key turning point was when I began to understand the power of metaphors and the impact these can have on the unconscious mind. Working with one of Steve's colleagues, the wonderful Gail Gibson, we looked at a powerful analogy that related to my situation. We went into an imaginary garden and planted seeds. In this visualisation the seeds had to be nurtured, fed and nourished so they would grow over time. They would start to poke their heads through the soil and look around and ultimately grow stronger into the kind of sturdy plant, capable of supporting itself and flowering each year. OK,

for many that's a simple analogy... but sometimes it's these simple things that you draw comfort from when you're in a dark place. This scenario stayed with me and little did I know I would soon be learning much more about metaphors and the power of the unconscious mind in yet another twist.

Strange things then started to happen and **one of the key learning points for me was the importance of doing 'something positive' and taking action, because you will then create a ripple of some kind in the universe.** *That may sound a bit cliché but that's precisely what happened. Do something positive and it will have a knock-on effect elsewhere. This is just like Steve advocates in Step 6 of his Career Navigation Cycle process 'taking positive action'.*

During my coaching programme with Steve's company, he started to write his first book 'Winning Through Redundancy – Six Steps to Navigate Your Way to A Brighter Future'. Steve was having a number of challenges with his initial publisher. He shared these with me – I was naturally interested in the subject and the book as they directly resonated with me."

The power of feedback

"I gave him feedback on some of the ideas, concepts and design work, so he then gave me the first chapter to read through. I offered comments with constructive criticism and I remember thinking 'some of this is out of sequence, out of order'. Steve was very pleased with my feedback and gave me the second chapter to critique. However, I couldn't see the transition from chapter one to two.

I remember going to Steve's house and we did a couple of enormous mind maps on the day. The process really started to unlock what the book was about, where it was going, what the chapters truly meant. This was really exciting and the end result was a much more cohesive and flowing book.

As this approach had worked so well, I ended up doing mind maps for all the other chapters of the book. Steve shared them with his illustrator, Tara, who was already inspired by what Steve was looking to achieve with his book. She used the mind maps as the basis to draw images, using her creative and artistic talents, to add value to Steve's writing.

So, yet again, something strange was happening here. What started as some initial feedback for Steve on his book was now becoming a wonderful collaborative project in which I was playing my part! Subsequently, I mentioned to people I had helped Steve write his first book and that it became internationally acclaimed and featured in the top 10 business books on Amazon. Their reaction was 'That's funny, I want to write a book... could you help me too?'

One woman in particular had asked people to critique her book; she had received nothing but glowing positive feedback from her friends and family. She wasn't convinced about the feedback so asked me if I would have a look at her manuscript. I did and I sent her back an extensive Word document with significant tracked changes all the way through. It was highly critical but in a constructive way. She was delighted as she didn't want people to tell her how great it was – she wanted an impartial objective viewpoint. She wanted to be challenged to help her seriously think again about the content of the book. A number of other people have since asked if I can help them write their books.

For Steve's second book, 'Winning Through Career Change', he asked me to be his copy and content editor. I also helped him again in reviewing all content, flow and creative ideas – just as I have done with this book. So, yet again I have now established another income stream and strand to my portfolio career.

I know I have always been a stickler for detail and that this was often an implied criticism. I've always maintained that 'the devil is in the detail' and consequently I have been able to produce consistently high quality results. I had also obviously taken my creative and problem solving skills for granted as new solutions were valued for the most challenging of problems. In no time I had earned the nickname of 'Sherlock' and the proud reputation that name evokes. Being able to do work I love, with people I admire and respect has been greatly rewarding. Collaborating with Steve to help him write an even more compelling book, and getting paid for it, has given me immense pleasure."

We will meet Steve again in Chapter 5, when looking at the re-design phase of a portfolio career and to see just how those *ripples* extend even further with ever increasing circles.

Key Learning Points from Steve's story

- It's surprising what other people see in you that you may not see yourself

- Undertaking new work and doing new things with new people will allow you to discover personal skills and abilities you may have either overlooked or taken for granted

- Positive feedback and feeling valued will build your confidence and provide the motivation to continue towards even greater aspirations

- Saying 'yes' to something new and unfamiliar is likely to feel daunting and uncomfortable, but is the quickest and most rewarding way to learn, gain a great sense of achievement and overcome your fears

- Reframing a situation is very powerful and allows us to challenge and change the statements that we make about our experience the world and to 'let go'

- Reframe the situation to realise 'what else could it positively mean?'

- Reframing a perceived threat can then appear as an opportunity. As in Steve's case a 'redundancy' could mean a new start in life and an 'opportunity' to do what you love

- Just do something positive and *create that ripple in the universe!*

The importance of reframing your thinking to achieve a fulfilling working lifestyle cannot be underestimated, as we will continue to explore in this next section.

Why Be Unhappy for 100K Hours?

Did you know that 100K hours is the average time you will spend at work, during your life? Think about how large that number is. Think about how many waking hours that means you will be at work, doing your job, day in, day out…

Now ask yourself, "Am I happy doing the work I'm doing? Is my job the *best* reason why I get out of bed every day? Do I love what I am doing?"

Research consistently shows that around 50% of working adults in the UK, US and other parts of the globe, are unhappy in their jobs and are looking for a more fulfilling career and lifestyle. There are varied reasons, with many citing boredom, not being valued, not achieving their potential, lack of career prospects, lack of development or worse still… a toxic working environment.

Are you one of the unhappy 50%?

If you are unhappy in your career, consider the prospect of continuing to work for 100K hours in your current role. How does that make you feel? Chances are you will experience these symptoms on a regular basis:

- Fearful on a Sunday evening about having to go to work on Monday morning

- Dread on a Monday morning because you don't want to go to work

- Worry and restlessness at work from Monday to Friday because you simply don't want to be there

- Ignoring the little voice inside your head saying "It's time to change"

Recognise yourself?

Lebanese philosopher, Kahlil Gibran quotes: *"If you cannot work with love but only with distaste, it is better that you should leave your work*". When we look at the high level of unhappiness among working adults, this quote rings so true. Instead of getting paid to be unhappy, why not listen to that little voice inside your head and bring about change in your work and life?

Take control of your career by changing what you do and get paid to be happy!

"That's all well and good", I hear you say, "but I have bills to pay, a family to keep and the cost of living keeps rising." So, is now the ideal time to change your career? What if you grin and bear it, remain unhappy, and receive your salary at the end of each month? At least this will pay the bills and keep your family, won't it?

However, reflect on the 100K hours of work statistic. Do you honestly want to spend that length of time of your life in a constant state of unhappiness? Consider how this will impact on you and others? Are you afraid to take a leap of faith to change and do fulfilling work you love? **Life is too short and there are so many amazing alternatives.**

The only way you will change how you feel about your work or career is to have the courage to follow your heart. Perhaps it's a change of scenery, people or time for you to embrace something in your life you are truly passionate about… just as you have seen with Don, Feza, Tara and Steve. This can be an opportune moment to realise your lifetime ambition. Give yourself a chance to do what you love and love what you do!

Walk away from your unhappiness

As with all the case studies and examples in this book, only you can make it happen. It's up to you to create an escape plan and to break free of the tedium. **You have the choice to do this.** But what about your financial situation when you give up your well paid salary?

Many people who are dissatisfied, disillusioned and unproductive at work are often those who earn the most money. In contrast, for many of my clients and people I know who have taken the leap of faith and discovered happiness in their work and career; it's not about the money. Happiness, purpose and fulfilment far outweigh the big pay cheque at the end of the month. *Why*? Because they have all reframed their thinking and are now working for the 3 Ps of Passion, Pleasure and Profit by doing what they love. What could be better than this?

So, how can you move from unhappiness to happiness in your career? Take a high dose of self-belief, reframe and say to yourself *'Now is my time to do what I love'*, and just do it!

Just think what you can do with the gift of 86,400 seconds (one day) to get started on your road to happiness.

📖 *Case Study: Jane's Story (Part 1)*

'Stop and question what life is all about'

"One of my key skills is being a change agent, yet I hadn't realised how difficult it is to change yourself!"

Jane Seeley is a wonderful example that showcases exactly why you must take action if you are unhappy in your job or career.

When I first met Jane she had reached an impasse with her career. She had reached the intersection at the crossroads and didn't know which way to turn. By her own admission she was a highly confident person who had always achieved whatever she set out to. She had developed her career to a high executive level in a global plc, was previously full of energy and ideas and always had a sense of purpose. As a result of key changes within the company she found herself confronted with the challenges of a new job and a new boss. This was not a role she felt comfortable or happy doing as she was not playing to her undoubted strengths. Her new boss had a completely different mindset and values to what she was accustomed to. Jane was also spending an inordinate amount of time travelling and being away from her family; something that she was finding increasingly uncomfortable at a time when her children were approaching major exams.

For the first time in her career Jane started to feel very differently about her company and was rapidly losing her confidence, energy and self-esteem. As difficult as it was for her, she knew that if she could not get back into a role that she wanted, she would have to leave and move on as her situation was becoming untenable.

Jane could not see herself moving to a competitor and it became clear she liked the idea of being her own boss. She even had a 'patchy' vision for starting her own company. However, her biggest concern and main reason for contacting me was clear from her statement, *"I don't know how I will survive without the corporate umbrella around me"*.

Reframing fear into focus

What I discovered, through coaching Jane, was that **fear** was at the heart of what was really holding her back. In fact it was a range of fears, e.g. a fear of the unknown, a fear of failure (something she had never experienced), a fear of not being able to reposition or reinvent herself, a fear of damaging her personal brand and a fear of not being able to earn enough.

Jane was astounded when I told her I had gone through all these self-doubts and fears myself; so had most of my clients. But were her fears perceptions or reality? Jane had proven throughout her career that once she had a goal, real focus, clarity and belief, she was capable of achieving anything. Moreover, her thinking was clearly an emotional response and a distorted perception rather than reality. From experience I know this to be the case with most people facing similar situations.

With this is mind, I coached Jane to help her reframe her fear and turn this into real focus. As a result, she regained her confidence, self-belief and sense of purpose and son began moving forward. In her words, *"The clouds lifted and my dark world turned into a glorious bright future. Don't delay, turn your fear into focus and take charge of your own future by doing something you love"*.

Jane then set up her own consultancy, which has since evolved into a number of different business ventures. She has become a highly sought-after business and IT change consultant, programme manager, coach and mentor. **Most importantly Jane has long banished her fears to become the architect of her own future, now living life on her terms and has never been happier.**

Now meet Jane and learn about her initial transition into a portfolio career.

Why did I leave the corporate world?

"For a number of reasons. I guess a big wakeup call happened on the basis I was travelling an awful lot and not seeing much of the family. Also, the company had grown into a corporate monster! **The values of the company had changed and they were really at odds with my own values, some of which were deep-rooted. This troubled me as it felt wrong having to compromise them.**

So, for probably 25 years I had a really exciting career, changed roles many times, worked my way up the organisation and enjoyed every year of it. But thereafter it all fell flat. I just wanted to do something different. My last role actually had elements of starting up businesses, so it gave me an understanding of how the concept worked, albeit for somebody else. However, they were making a lot of money out of my expertise, so I came round to thinking that perhaps I should do something for myself instead."

How did I start my own business?

"The last project I worked on for the organisation was something called 'cold-chain', which I became quite passionate about. This is effectively ensuring stability of temperature controlled products during transport to varied climates over extended durations. I felt quite strongly the industry wasn't moving forward fast enough. So, I spent quite a lot of time looking at how I could position myself in that market with products and services, through the network that I had gained in my corporate life.

I started down this road in my new life as a business owner. Interestingly my first big project was actually in IT consulting. I was asked to take on a programme that wasn't going to plan, for a company headed up by somebody I had previously worked for. They knew I had the required skills and asked me 'to go in and rescue it', which I did.

Word soon got around I was now doing IT consulting, so my phone was hot with calls asking me to consider new projects. Most of my work came as a result of word-of-mouth recommendations, together with referrals from people I knew through my extended business networks. People who understood my skill set, my previous experience and who wanted somebody to solve their problems. Ironically this was often to help people embrace organisational change. **One of my key skills is being a change agent, yet I hadn't realised back then just how difficult it is to change yourself."**

How has my portfolio career evolved?

"My plans for the cold-chain work took a back seat as the IT consulting really took off. Interestingly, alongside this work there were growing assignments to provide coaching, mentoring and leadership development for managers. This was probably due to my previous management experience.

In addition, having previously looked after and hosted football academy students, my husband and I decided to explore foster caring. So, I have also added respite fostering to my portfolio as well.

My portfolio is not only about people, but also providing technical frameworks and models to help improve and develop IT services and operational performance. I really enjoy having the different elements. My portfolio strands all offer something different. IT consulting keeps me involved in the corporate camp. This is great because I really enjoy working with companies, understanding their strategy, their growth and where they are heading.

My main interest in the cold-chain work is to ensure that there's no waste in the food-chain.

Foster caring is just nice to give something back. Likewise, you get the overwhelming feeling of satisfaction that you have provided support and guidance to a young person. Above all it helps ground you and remind you what is important in life. It makes you realise, or stop and question, what life is all about.

I've also been involved in a number of other projects and business ventures, including coaching footballers who either fail to make the grade, or have reached the end of their careers. Unfortunately, this has proven a really difficult market to tap into."

Blending work and life

"Having a portfolio career has given me the opportunity to take up new hobbies I would never have had time for in the corporate world. I have developed a real passion for canal boating and it's so stress-free. This is something that my husband and I enjoy so much, that we've challenged our whole thinking around what we really need and want to do with our lives. Perhaps we should retire early and just give up everything we've worked for to get a totally new blend of life that is actually within our reach now. However, I don't think I will ever fully retire and I can certainly see there's another chapter looming and new opportunities for me to add to my portfolio career."

Key Learning Points from Jane's story

- If you have reached a career crossroads It pays to be honest with yourself and take stock

- Deep rooted values compromised by an employer suggest it's time to move on and change

- Even you do work helping people or organisations to change, it isn't easy to change yourself

- Getting the right professional help will enable you to reframe and overcome your fears to achieve new career and life goals you may not have thought possible

- Do not underestimate the reputation you have developed in your employed life – it will put you in good stead if you start doing something in your own right, as a business owner

- By managing your networks effectively, word will get around quickly you are in the market for different aspects of work you do in your new portfolio career

- You will always be in demand if you have the right skills, experience and importantly the right mindset to solve other people's problems

- Whatever your initial business plans were, people will quickly gravitate to you for work they perceive you are best at, so don't let this stifle your need for variety in your portfolio

- Having a portfolio career can help you to find the time to discover new hobbies and passions

Final Thoughts

Reframing will help you change your perspective and lens to the world. In order to change, you must first change your thinking… change your thinking and you can ultimately change your life. This is why the *'toolkit for life'* is a great mantra to follow. If you are one of the unhappy 50%, a portfolio career and working for the 3 Ps is one of the amazing alternatives open to you.

There are many myths about portfolio careers, but the reality is very different. Moreover, if you never take the leap of faith you will never find out! As we have seen, some passions will never pay enough but follow the 3 Cs approach to take control of your career and find fulfilment doing work you love.

Steve and Jane's case studies highlight the importance of regularly taking stock and questioning what is important in your career and life. By doing so you can also discover and achieve your right working lifestyle blend.

We will meet Jane again in Chapter 5 to learn how by focusing on the 3 Cs, her portfolio career journey has continued to change course in a very different and fascinating way.

Now move onto Chapter 4 to *'rediscover your happy place'* and meet some people who have already made challenging breakthroughs to do so.

CHAPTER 4

Rediscover – Have You Forgotten Your Happy Place?

"So come with me, where dreams are born, and time is never planned. Just think of happy things, and your heart will fly on wings, forever, in Never Land!" – Peter Pan

As you are about to embark on a possible new venture in your career and life, it is helpful to become aware of positive influences from your past that made you happy, to bring these forward with you. It is time to free up your thinking and cast aside unwanted aspects of your working lifestyle. Moving forward now, establishing your personal values and needs will allow you to find and stay true to your authentic self. These will form a solid foundation on which to build a fulfilling portfolio career.

Finding your happy place

You can trace the origins of J. M. Barrie's character, Peter Pan, way back to 1902 as 'the boy who never grew up'. However, the 1991 movie called 'Hook' featured an adult Peter Pan who had to return to Neverland to win back his children previously stolen by Captain Hook. Peter's task was to re-engage with his child side, his 'happy place', in order to challenge his old enemy.

Take a look at Peter Pan in this adult character role. Peter is no longer in touch with his inner child, the place where he was happiest. In this 'happy place' Peter was able to let go of the stresses and strains of being an adult and he gave himself an opportunity to free his thinking. 'Letting go' gave Peter the belief and skill to defeat his enemy and take his children home.

How does visiting your 'happy place' relate to transitioning into a portfolio career?

Good question. Having transitioned to become a successful career coach, I got to wondering what the key ingredients were for winning through career and life changes. This resulted in developing my six step Career Navigation Cycle. The proven successful process consists of six sequential stages. Each stage of the process was purposely designed to help people to challenge themselves and progress incrementally in achieving what they want in life, i.e. their career, working lifestyle, goals and dreams. What is abundantly clear is **the importance to focus on what you want (that will make you happy and fulfilled) and not what you don't want or what you fear.**

I have already stated the first step to change is to change yourself by 'letting go'. Just like the examples of Steve and Jane in Chapter 3, many people find themselves in unfamiliar territory when circumstances suddenly change following a long period of steady employment. As you have seen, letting go and visiting their 'happy place' was almost like discovering a new planet. The same may also be true for you, but wouldn't it be great to find out?

Before you can take a positive step, you must let go of what you thought you knew

If you have made a decision to leave your job, or even your career, stop for a moment to consider what led to that decision. Maybe it was to realise your passions or perhaps you felt it was just time for a change? Either way, you are now about to set sail on a new voyage of self-discovery. You've raised the anchor, hoisted the sails and your view is focused on the horizon. You are ready to embrace a new and exciting opportunity and create a working lifestyle of your dreams!

Rather than sailing headlong into stormy weather, you must take the step of 'letting go' to allow you to reach your 'happy place'. It's your chance to dispel thoughts, unwind and release your conditioned past. Like Peter Pan, you can go 'where dreams are born'.

Free your thoughts and your mind will open itself to greater opportunity

In this vital stage of career transition you need to devote time to just 'be' and not 'do'. This may sound all rather spiritual and people often link it to a state of inner peace, a self-awareness or mindfulness. This state is far from being passive as the cleansing that takes place can often lead to great productivity. Imagine what would have happened if Peter Pan had not allowed himself to 'be' in his 'happy place'? His children would have remained forever more with Captain Hook. Allow yourself to re-engage with your inner child. Open your mind like a sponge and become absorbed in just 'being'.

Let go to just 'be' and not 'do' to inspire your own self-belief so that 'your heart will fly on wings, forever, in Never Land'.

Is it time for a change of scenery?

Let's say you take a chance on your career. You change tack, take a gamble and you go 'off-piste'. How does this level of uncertainty sit with you? Does the unknown fill you with dread, worry and concern? Or, does it shout opportunity, excitement and fun? The latter is all about daring to be different; to be flexible in approach and meet new challenges and change head on.

Just with many of the case studies in this book, and with my own adventure, the future can be both scary and exciting.

"What will happen to my career? Where will my journey lead me?" you may ask. On the other hand, what will happen to you if you continue on your current unhappy and unfulfilled linear career path?

Are you prepared to go off-piste?

Imagine you are standing on your skis at the top of the mountain. You are faced with the choice of two possible paths to descend. One is clearly mapped out and is a well-used favourite run for most skiers. The other is obscure; an uncharted route that requires you to go 'off-piste'.

Which way will you go?

Consider for a moment what you will see on the mapped out path. The winding run will no doubt be picturesque with snow covered pines and breath-taking views across the valley. As you ski down this path you will follow the existing grooves in the snow; a path already skied, time and again, by those before you.

Imagine just how different your run can be when you go off-piste? 'Off-piste' says 'risk', 'unknown' and deviates from the conventional. It's a path less skied. Who knows what you'll discover along the way?

Rethink the model of what your career path can look like

Think broadly. Allow yourself an unrestricted view of the snow-capped mountains. Fasten your skis, open your mind and choose a new path; the one less skied. Go off-piste and enjoy a new found freedom and choice in your career and the work you do. This could be your new portfolio career!

Becoming the architect of your own future

In Chapter 3 we looked at examples of what many people say they want to change in their careers and lives. By becoming the architect of your own future, you will be making a conscious decision to take back control of your career and life. You can now start to create an exciting new portfolio career and working lifestyle based on your choices. But there is always a compromise or trade-off, isn't there?

Right at the start of the book, we looked at giving up the dreaded daily commute, which I'm sure many of you would be willingly do too. However, in order to change your working lifestyle, the route to success is rarely straightforward and you may need to navigate obstacles and barriers along the way.

For example, when considering a move to find to your new dream home, it is often rare to find a house that exactly matches everything on your list of 'wants' and 'needs'. Although I am not suggesting this will always be the case, you do need to consider the implications of moving from your current career to designing a portfolio career if you choose to go 'off-piste'. You will have to make some tough and important decisions and there will inevitably be some compromises.

What are you prepared to trade to be happy?

At the time of writing this section I became involved in a LinkedIn group discussion about whether people would be willing to take a pay cut to move towards a dream job? From the perspective of this book, the 'dream job' could mean the creation of a portfolio career of choice. *How do you think most people answered?*

Interestingly, the vast majority of people's answers were consistent with research conducted over the last decade. Such research invariably showed that 'high earners' were happy to trade some of their salary in order to achieve the working lifestyle they wanted and to do work they loved.

In my experience it is clear that most people, regardless of being a 'high earner', are quite prepared to take a reduction in salary to achieve a new working lifestyle. There are of course caveats and people still need to ensure that can continue to support their families without making too many sacrifices. *We therefore come back to the 'reframe' as mentioned in Chapter 3, i.e. to change and reframe your mindset from one of consistently receiving a high income, to one of 'earning enough'.*

So what, if anything, are you prepared to trade to achieve the working lifestyle you now desire? Consider this question carefully as it is highly significant. *Why?...* Because, your answers will now start to reshape your thinking and focus for the future.

Typical examples of what you might be prepared to trade:

- Previous career aspirations, e.g. management, senior management or top executive

- 'High salary' – you may already be earning somewhere close to your aspiration, but are prepared to earn less to change your working lifestyle

- Regular salary – knowing when and how much you get paid each month

- Paid holidays

- Company Pension Scheme

- Certain company benefits

- Job security (does that really exist today?)

Ultimately, changing your mindset and perception will help you overcome any fears you may have in making compromises in these examples, or any other aspects of employed life.

The Emotional Roller Coaster

As with many of the case studies in this book, your new approach and outlook on life is likely to be turbulent; something I have likened to an emotional roller coaster ride. There could be many twists and turns and unexpected highs and lows. The amazing Tara Winona (Chapter 2) helped me create a wonderful image to depict this for my *'Winning Through Career Change'* book. In view of its relevance, and to help you grasp the significance, I am featuring it again:

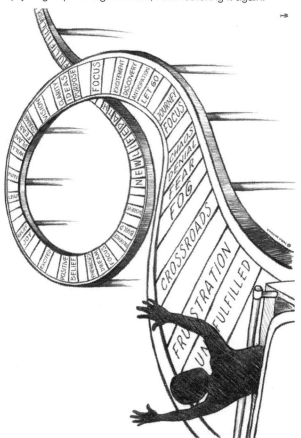

📖 *Case Study: Julian's Story*

A job that allows you to 'dance with other opportunities'

"I have a life that works as long as it flexes and that's what a portfolio career does for me"

"A fundamental aspect of any successful portfolio career is to ensure that you don't put all your eggs in one basket. Having a broader range of options enables you to lessen any potential risk, whilst also creating more choice and variety in the work you do."

Let's now meet *Julian Childs,* a most interesting character, a great advocate of the portfolio career and someone who wisely avoids concentrating all efforts and resources in one area. I have known Julian for a number of years and we have a mutual respect for each other and the work we do. Julian is also a wonderful example of someone who has had to rediscover himself and his happy place on more than one occasion. Julian has certainly also seen the highs and lows of employed, unemployed, self-employed and portfolio life. He has taken many rides on the emotional roller coaster as you will come to see.

Background

"I was a 'yuppie' in the city of London and worked in financial services advertising. When recession in the early 90's hit advertising budgets of our big financial institutional clients, I was an account director and an expensive asset on the payroll. I was in the first wave of redundancy, which was good because they paid me more than they would have done later on. I think they were embarrassed at that time about redundancy, but then they stopped being embarrassed about it. So back in the early '90s I was thrown out of the employment market.

I spent best part of two years backpacking, spending my redundancy money and more that I had earned casually along the way, because I had no job to come back to. I came back to the UK and tried to get a job. I had three interviews for a marketing director role. I was pitching high, but didn't get offered the job and was broke."

My Reframe

"I pondered, 'what's the difference between me as a successful employee, and me as an unemployed professional?' I thought the difference was I didn't have a brand to represent. So, I reckoned that if I created a brand and started talking about myself as 'we', i.e. 'we do this' and 'we do that', there was no reason why I couldn't replicate the success I had had before as an employee. That's what I did. I did it through the marketing agency that I created. I called it 'Mainly Marketing'. It took two years to really get off the ground. I struggled for a couple of years and then it flew."

Think like an entrepreneur

"I had to become instantly very resourceful because there was no paymaster except me. I had to generate the work and then do it. That forces you to become opportunistic. It gives you an impetus to become entrepreneurial, look for opportunities, to make links and associations, to notice things other people just don't and to go for them speculatively.

The portfolio bit came about because I was speculatively, simultaneously trying after all sorts of things, unless I was already so snowed under with work that I couldn't. That's a nice problem to have but it leads to another problem, which is a lull afterwards when you've got through the hiatus. I became adept at offering to do things, offering to look at things, consider things, consult on things, advise on things. I was also doing some voluntary work with Crisis, the homeless charity. That was probably the extent of my portfolio career at that stage."

How did my Portfolio career evolve?

"My portfolio career developed by expedience, rather than conscious. I focused on it deliberately when I couldn't get a job, as I said I was pitching high. My CV said I had a good track record and yet I wasn't landing jobs. I think fundamentally my values had changed during my travels. I was less employable in the conventional sense. I was too questioning, too independent, too resilient. People could see that and probably with fewer freelancers and portfolio type people around, they were also suspicious of anybody who had either the goal or the opportunity to climb a few mountains, or retreat to a few beaches for long term. Basically, I didn't fit with the conventional job market anymore! So, I had to invent my own business and then, in trying to feed myself through my own business, I became adept at trying lots of things simultaneously.

My portfolio career has still evolved and I guess I am very lucky. I have an employed position these days. It evolved out of a part-time freelance role. I'm a career coach and business advisor at a beautiful private university in Regents Park, London. I also have other strands to my portfolio as I will share. So, I have a job and other self-employed and businesses."

My typical Portfolio week

"Ostensibly, that's five days a week, full-time, salaried, pensioned, holidayed, all those wonderful perks. However, when it was offered to me I was quite hesitant after 20 years of self-employment. I didn't want them to clip my wings.

I made that very clear because my portfolio life works as no one's looking over my shoulder. Things can ripple into each other, overlap, creating possibilities. Whereas, if you have to respect a rigid employed, salaried position with set hours and responsibilities, they won't allow you to talk to anybody else; you're fundamentally restricted in possibility. My employer at Regent's University London said: 'We get that. We want you because of your ability to dance with other opportunities and the opportunities that also creates for us. So just keep doing what you do. We've got targets for you, and you will have to answer to those, but as long as you do that, you can approach the job how you wish. We trust you and we like you.'

It works well, so I am grateful for that. My work at Regent's University is career coaching and business advising for international graduates and post-grads; mostly post-graduates and early years alumni. In addition, I have a shareholding and directorship interest in a recruitment business called 'Talentfield'.

Essentially, we supply senior, marketing talent on a short term contract basis. The fact the market can exist is a reflection of this portfolio age. It doesn't take much of my time and it also allows me to monetize my networking activities and career coaching with senior marketers. I have an irregular flow because I don't market myself aggressively for this work, but I have private clients who come to me from my reputation, by recommendation or because they've worked with me in the past. They need a 'repeat prescription', so that's great. I've also finished studying for a master's degree.

*Beyond that I like the great outdoors, socialising, I have a few family responsibilities and a nice home. **I have a life that works as long as it flexes and that's what a portfolio career and lifestyle does for me."***

Riding the emotional roller coaster!

"Previously, I had spent nine years building up a pretty successful business and then ten months losing it. That was painful. My losses ran into six figures. But more than that, it was my business, my baby, my creation. I was very proud of it and to lose it was shocking, horrible. I was very angry and very aggrieved.

For the next year or so I took things easy again. I realised I wasn't making good decisions and I needed to get my equilibrium back. I did some interesting, speculative and low-stress things. They ranged from selling Christmas hampers at Fortnum & Mason to being a guide at Down House, which is Charles Darwin's old home, now run by English Heritage. They were paid roles.

I also worked over the summer as a volunteer guide on a whale-watching study boat in Tenerife. I cycled the length of the River Thames in order to put strength in my legs, as part of the training for tackling Wainwright's 'Coast-to-Coast Walk'. So, I had a lovely time and I recovered my sense of being 'happy'.

At the end of that period, I wrote to all my old clients and explained that I've had the time out that I needed, I'm back but I don't have an appetite to rebuild the original marketing agency. I basically put out the message that I would consider anything and would be grateful for any work, if it felt right."

The Upswing

"Looking back, maybe this was a strange thing to do. However, within the first morning of that email going out, two of my old clients had contacted me to ask if I would come in part-time freelance, to run marketing projects for them. Essentially, this meant doing work I had a history

of doing without any responsibility for staff. I just had to rock up. I was quickly on good money again and it was so much easier than running my own agency. I thought this was brilliant!"

The big dip

"That feeling only lasted a couple of years though. It gradually evolved into feast and famine. I was either head down, doing project work for other people, or head up looking for the next one. But I couldn't be doing both at once. So, I had backed myself into a corner where I wasn't doing work that I particularly enjoy, or was in a position to choose. I was also working for people whose only 'thank you' was paying me promptly and well. They never said thank you, because I wasn't employed staff.

I suppose I hit some kind of midlife crisis. I was early forties then, but I just ran out of steam. I had no enthusiasm for what I was doing and I was fed up with it. If you would have asked me at that stage what I wanted to do, I would have said, 'anything but this.'

I didn't know what I wanted. I was just confused and lost. I hired a career coach and I did a lot of personal development reading. I went on a lot of long walks, retreats and things like that to just try and think things through. I do remember it was a very uncomfortable time. I was deeply uncertain about anything, questioning and challenging everything that was familiar.

But then interesting and formative things happened. I was given an opportunity to pitch for a marketing project for a charity. I won that pitch and that was fascinating to me. It was in fact not really a charity, it was a social enterprise; the business end of a charity. An alternative to fundraising is that you have a trading entity that generates an income to support the charity. I got myself very quickly swept up and involved with the project and became a lead in fundraising. I won a big lottery grant to set up a chain of second-hand furniture shops; selling furniture we had collected from people getting rid of it. This saved it from landfill. We sold it in four pilot shops using staff who were marginalised in some way; people with learning difficulties, criminal records, socially excluded etc. Teach them customer service, teach them merchandising skills, teach them delivery logistics, and they became valuable, very valuable. We were mimicking a business we had seen in Belgium under a brand name we created for the UK, M-O-R-P-H. We transitioned things and people from 'rubbish into treasure'. We asked Big Lottery for several million pounds more to open up a whole chain of shops across the UK. Unfortunately, they said no as it wasn't the right time. Great Britain had won the Olympic bid and all the money that was going into the charity sector had been swept into that pot. So, having opened four shops we had to make 20 people redundant and close three of them.

It's a long story but I had a false start. I thought I was becoming a social enterprise entrepreneur but it was short-lived. It lasted about a year and a half. In the process I only got paid when I was able to raise funds for the project. By following my heart, I had built up a substantial private debt. It was an interesting journey but not clever."

Another twist and turn

"I used to do side line work and one aspect was lecturing on marketing for small businesses. I was drawing on previous experience by running workshops for start-ups around London, sponsored by Chambers of Commerce. One day, a lady on my course came up to me afterwards and said how much she had enjoyed it and what she learned. She said I had an interesting story and I would make a good outplacement coach. What was 'outplacement'? I didn't know what it was. I now know that it is career coaching for people who have been made redundant. It turned out she worked part time for one of the big firms in London. She said they were looking for part-time freelancers and she could introduce me to her boss."

The power of introductions and referrals

"I had a coffee with her boss who said, they were very interested because I understood self-employment and the charity sectors. These were both options that people who had been affected by redundancy from the corporate sector would often consider as alternatives. He said, 'You can teach them about that with credibility and we will teach you about CV writing, job applications, marketing letters and interview skills.'

So, very unexpectedly, I fell into that. I absolutely didn't know such roles existed. Furthermore, within weeks I knew I could do it well. It was a wonderful, joyful thing to find something in my mid-forties that I just fell into and I fitted. It was a very good fit and still is."

A big upswing

"Fast forwarding and linking the story to the future, I did outplacement work in Mayfair for senior executives for over three years. One of my colleagues won a large contract delivering career coaching to MBA students at Leeds University Business School. She had a portfolio career and this project was way too big for her to deliver on her own, so she asked if I could help her. I said, 'I don't know the first thing about coaching MBAs'. She said, 'Well it's like outplacement, but you don't have to pick them up off the floor first.'

This was very accurate. Young, talented, bright, challenging, ambitious people are joyful to work with! They're naive, they're wet behind the ears and they need help, but they're also pushing all the time and that's really great. So, on the back of a year at Leeds which was great fun, but inconvenient when you live in Kent, I enquired around London and got a freelance contract at the wonderful Regent's University. So that's how things fell into place."

What have been my biggest challenges?

"I wouldn't say it's been smooth at any stage. I think the first challenge was to 'learn to ride'. Learn to just rock and roll with whatever you're dealing with. Sometimes life can be easier than other times and you've just got to know that circumstances always be so difficult. When faced with such disappointments, the challenge is being able maintain your self-reliance and resilience; then you will be able to cope with them.

Cash-flow has also been a major challenge at various stages of my journey. I was working at Regent's University London for three years, part-time freelance, between two and four days a week depending on what they needed. So, my income could fluctuate a lot in that time. The challenge was managing cash-flow, dependency and the 'legs of my portfolio stool'. If you say 'yes' to too much from one basket it can knock the stool over. So that was a challenge to learn and manage.

Conversely, making plans around freelance work when it's suddenly cut and you're not expecting that, can render you 'on holiday without a budget' very quickly.

Cash-flow is king. It's king in any business and where there's portfolio work in your business."

Making trade-offs

"Now that I'm salaried, I have dependable, predictable income. It comes in on approximately the same date every month and that's nice. I can sleep better for the certainty, but it also blocks my diary significantly. Therefore, it reduces my flexibility and opportunity to change my income dramatically. So it's a trade-off. That's a challenge too.

Now I've found something I love to do, in a place I love to do it, that's great. However, I have in the past found myself saying 'yes' to projects or people I really was not best equipped to deal with, just because I needed the income. You've got to be adept at managing relationships in that situation and you've got to be compartmentalising your thoughts. 'I don't really like this work' or 'I don't really like that person' is a means to an end; it's an expedient way to think. It might only be short-term but it's still a challenge."

What have I learnt from my portfolio journey?

"I've learnt that variety is a valuable spice of life. It's not just variety is the spice of life, but it's that variety that keeps you interested and interesting and provides new possibilities if you are open to see them. I've learnt that I'm actually a pretty good time-manager and I'm a pretty good multitasker. I don't think an employer has ever told me either of those things, but I've learnt that I can count on those things. I've also learnt to trust my own intuition or internal panic button. I can somehow automatically realise what's urgent and it doesn't trouble me until it needs to.

A freelancer I used to work with in the world of advertising over 20 years ago (he was freelancing and I was salaried at the time) told me, 'The most important thing was to build a pot of drop-dead money'. This is essentially a buffer that allows you to say 'no' to any work that you don't want to do, and to even walk away from anything that you're not enjoying. I never did that and I have ended up, as a consequence, quite often doing work that I didn't like.

I would trust that when you find things that you thoroughly enjoy, you are, in my experience, usually pretty good at them. So I would invest more time in looking for things that I enjoyed. I would pursue them for their longer term possibilities, rather than going after anything just because it was an earning opportunity.

I used to think that big salaried people were safe and secure. The more I see in life, the older I get and the more senior the people I mix with, has all helped me realise they're as vulnerable as the next person, and often more so. They are so conspicuously expensive."

What would I do differently, if I had my time again?

"Trusting my intuition, following your nose, really. I'd probably do more charity work early on, although that sounds a very decent and wholesome thing to do. Actually it's those situations where you are giving, that make you appreciate better what you're good at and valued for.

It's good to stay grounded around people who are not necessarily as privileged as you might be. I think it brings you closer to your heart, it's that simple. It brings you into contact with situations and people where you feel empathy and that can be useful. It can also generate earning opportunities as well.

The biggest stress I've had in recent years is when that balance is out of kilter. I've had to keep going despite the balance not being a healthy one. So, I would seek work-life balance.

I would seek to hang out with positive people. Negative people, naysayers, cautious people, they really do drain energy. They're alright in small doses, but I'd be very careful spending a lot of time with them. It's far better to surround yourself with people who've got a positive outlook and a focus of 'possibility'. They are exciting and fun people to hang out with."

What do I enjoy most about a portfolio career?

"I really fell into it. I was one of the first people I knew who actually had a portfolio that worked. I've coached a lot of people in recent years and a lot of them, especially once they reach middle years; find it a comfortable way to live.

What do I like about a portfolio career over a typical employed job? In summary, variety, possibility, a greater feeling of control; albeit it isn't always controlled or controllable but a greater feeling of fulfilling one's own agenda, rather than other people's. These are the key things I value the most about having a portfolio career and lifestyle."

Key Learning Points from Julian's story

- Not having all your eggs in one basket enables you to lessen any potential risk and create more choice and variety in the work you do

- Be opportunistic – think like an entrepreneur

- Try new things and your portfolio career could evolve by expedience

- Trust your intuition and be aware of your changing values and stay true to them

- Build up a financial buffer to make it easier to say 'no' to any work that you don't want to do

- By negotiating mutually beneficial terms, it's possible to have a full-time employed job plus other self-employed strands to your portfolio, to provide a mix of regular income and variety

- Your portfolio career can be an emotional roller coaster journey but learn to 'just rock and roll and ride'

- Introductions and referrals are absolutely the best way to gain new work

- Networking and talking to people is key – you never know who you will meet and who can unlock the key to your future by opening up an unexpected strand to your portfolio career

- Surround yourself with positive people who see excitement, fun and possibilities

- Cash flow is king – you have to keep the money flowing in otherwise you have no business!

Values – What is important to you in your career and life and WHY

Julian's fascinating case study highlights many great learning points. Moreover, there is a common theme emerging that is consistent with all the case studies featured throughout the book. *What is that theme?* **It is the importance of understanding and being true to your values.**

As you have seen with Julian's story, in our fast moving world and lives we rarely stop and reflect. Unless you are aware of the importance of reflection, and to 'be' rather than 'do', you are likely to just stumble through life. When we do take stock and challenge our thinking the result can be very powerful and poignant; just as we saw with Don and especially Tara in previous chapters. The same is absolutely true with your values.

Research over the last decade consistently shows that 1 in 2 people are in 'the wrong job' and 'unfulfilled'. This is startling to say the least and such people are effectively 'wage slaves'. We all know people who feel this way about their job; they spend their lives moaning and groaning about their company, boss etc.

You may have also feel this way, but don't understand why you do. Like most people, you may also feel this is perfectly normal and just ignore such feelings and get on with life. Unfortunately, the reality is that nothing will change unless you get to the root of your feelings. This is why only a small percentage of people ever take the leap of faith and change careers; it's so much easier to stay in your comfort zone, isn't it? However, this book is to help you challenge how you feel about work and life to enable you to lead a fulfilling working lifestyle of your choice, so let's dig deeper.

Values and Needs

We all have a set of values. These are the lasting beliefs we hold dear that affect our behaviour and allow us to lead an authentic life. We also have a set of needs. These are things that we must have in order to feel motivated and they contribute to our overall sense of wellbeing. Without understanding your career 'Values and Needs' it becomes almost impossible to find real meaning and fulfilment in when creating a portfolio career. This is quite fundamental when seeking out the right work that suits you. Therefore, when you feel unhappy or unfulfilled with your job/employer/career, then it's likely that you are out of synch with what you are doing and there is a direct conflict with your values and needs.

Now here's the thing. Once you understand your values and needs, you will establish what is important to you in your career and life and why you feel the way you do. **This is really powerful because once you have established your 'why', and you are clear about what is important to you, these factors will become your key drivers and call to action.**

What gets you out of bed each day?

No, not that old joke about your alarm clock or Smartphone!

- What is your motivation for getting up each day?

- What are the <u>must have</u> values and needs in your career and life?

The answers to these questions are important because they will provide some real clues as to why you want to work and what really gets you out of bed each day. Your career values and needs will often change over time but we rarely explore or even consider them.

What causes your values to change?

Changes to your values can happen either consciously or unconsciously as a result of key changes in your working life. For example:

- Promotion

- Redundancy (lay-off)

- Redeployment

- Organisational restructuring

- New ownership

- New boss

- New technology

Many people often begin to challenge the way they feel as a result of events or significant changes in their personal life. For example:

- Marriage

- Divorce

- Bereavement

- Having children

- Children leaving 'the nest'

- Becoming a grandparent

- Injury, major operations or other serious health issues

Challenging your values

In my case there have been at least two key times in my life when I have seriously challenged my values. The first occasion hit me big time following the death of my Father. I was considering rekindling my executive career at the time, but that suddenly felt hugely insignificant as there were far more important things in life. Not least, how on earth would my Mother cope without him as they had been 'joined at the hip' for over fifty years. *I realised that having more flexibility in my working life was something I now valued and needed.*

The second instance was during recuperation from major hip replacement surgery. Even though a number of my friends had previously had hip replacement operations, I had completely underestimated the impact this would have on me. Although I worked really hard at my physio exercises and to get enough mobility back to walk unaided, I was sapped of energy for weeks throughout that period. I could only work for a couple of hours before I needed to rest. However, things happen for a reason, don't they?

Only a few months earlier, I had achieved a lifelong ambition and become a published author of my first book *'Winning through Redundancy – Six steps to navigate your way to a brighter future'*. This was the climax of a real emotional roller coaster ride for me and a two-year labour of love. Having been thrilled and humbled to have been commissioned by a leading global publisher, which is very unusual for a new author, they let me down badly at the 11th hour and terminated my contract (by email) just as the book was about to be published.

Many people have told me I could probably write a book about writing that book, my journey and what I learned from the process. The initial publisher had ripped the guts out of my book and it had become a pale shadow of what I was looking to achieve. Although I was naturally very upset I was determined not to be derailed. I reframed and found a new publisher within 24 hours who promised to: *'publish the book I had always dreamt of, rather than what a major publisher wanted'*.

People were amazed at how I had managed to bounce back so quickly to achieve such a result, having been so badly let down. *How did I do this?* By walking my talk and following the same process and principles I have been sharing with you in this book, i.e. letting go, reframing and re-evaluating what I wanted to achieve to turn the negative situation into a positive new opportunity. I'm sure in developing your portfolio career you will also experience similar disappointments. Just when you thought you had secured a key project or piece of work, you may find your hopes are dashed at the final hurdle.

As you can too, I did achieve a happy ending. The book was bigger and better, published in a blaze of glory with an impactful new cover. It received brilliant reviews in the UK major national press and various business media, as well as from inspired readers around the globe. I was so proud to receive a glowing endorsement from the great Brian Tracy (American Internationally Renowned Speaker, Psychologist, Personal Development guru).

Looking back, I don't believe I ever realised just how much the whole experience had affected me emotionally. Nonetheless, it was clearly meant to be. Following my hip replacement, I had a huge amount of time to think, read, reflect and re-evaluate what I wanted from my working life.

Taking positive action from your learning

For years my wife and my best friend Don (see Chapter 1) had been telling me, to no avail, that 'I worked too hard'. Don even brought me a picture, an amusing cartoon of someone playing golf, as a metaphor to remind me I used to make time to play golf but I had barely played in years. Although it was my choice to work when and how I did, things had to change. Why did I need to work such long hours anyway? Maybe like you, or other people you know, it had just become habit rather than need?

In my reflective time I realised I was always banging on to other people about 'less being more', and how productivity could be improved by working less and freeing up time for leisure pursuits and hobbies. I needed to 'walk my talk' in this respect and to review my own portfolio career.

I decided I wanted to write more. I had been told by a top publicist who helped me greatly with my first book, I had at least five books in me over the next ten years. I needed to make the time to make it happen. You are reading number three and I already have plans for at least two more and still have four years to go!

As writing is a key part of my personal brand, it made sense to focus on developing my 'Steve Preston the Career Catalyst' brand as a leading career coach, author and speaker and to downsize how much time I spent on my company. It was also time for a serious rethink of what we wanted to achieve as a company then rebrand to achieve this new focus. The result… I'm now two books further down the line and we have a much more streamlined company offering that is focused on services that plays to the strength of our team. Most importantly, I have completely changed my working lifestyle.

Another key decision was to relearn to play the guitar again, after a 40-year break. I saw this as an opportunity to consciously make the time to be able to benefit and enjoy this interest for many years to come. Despite not being a natural musician (my tutor says who is?) and my learning curve definitely being an emotional roller coaster, I am enjoying the challenge and slowly but surely winning through. It has become a key part of my life. However, I know of at least a couple of people my age who have quit as they wanted a quick fix. **Like most things in life, there are rarely any shortcuts that work out and more haste = less speed. This same principle applies to creating your portfolio career of choice.**

Lastly, although I was already a keen tennis player, I wanted to prove my hip replacement would not hold me back. Three years on I am playing regular singles at least once a week, including competitively for the first time in years. Having seen the benefit of exercise to help my rehabilitation, I make sure I walk or cycle daily and always make time for my body balance class at the gym to improve my mobility. Many of these activities I now make time for during the working day and not just weekends or evenings. **I now view all these activities** as part of my weekly working lifestyle, which has been a massive reframe and mindset shift for me.

Your code to live by

So, why I am sharing some of my memoirs with you? Because, *your key values and needs will become the code that you should live by to lead an authentic and fulfilling life*. Once you understand your key values and needs and why they are so important to you, then you can reshape your career and re-design your working lifestyle, just as I have done all over again. Therefore, **uncovering your values and needs is the foundation to build upon, to change the way you work and earn!**

Examples of Values and Needs could be:

- Helping Others
- Independence
- Variety
- Challenge
- Earning 'enough'
- Flexibility

If you wish to <u>assess your career values and needs</u> to establish the 'must haves' in your career and life, do check out my video, and special Values Tool, to help you build the foundation to your portfolio career.

You will find details and a special reader offer at the back of the book in the *Inspirational Career & Personal Development Resources* section.

Case Study: Gail's Story (Part 1)

Finding your authentic self

Now meet Gail Gibson. For reasons which will become more apparent, you will read more about how I met Gail in the next chapter together with more of her story. Like me, Gail has long championed the merits of a portfolio career. How she discovered and embraced her portfolio career is a fascinating story which you may resonate with too, especially now we have explored values.

"Picture the scene. For some while I was unsettled and felt maybe it was my time to work toward my own goals and dreams. I had been working in a company for nine years and I was involved in learning and development with a large team all over the UK. I was sitting in our weekly management meeting and this particular one was going nowhere. In my mind it was an absolute waste of time. So I very quickly 'removed myself from the room' and took my mind elsewhere. I imagined I was sitting on my favourite beach in Malaysia. I could feel the sun on my skin; I could feel the water on my toes. I was a million miles away.

After the meeting the general manager called me into his office and he said, 'Gail, you weren't very present in the meeting today. You didn't have much to say'. So I told him it was a waste of my time and the managers' time. There was no focus or direction and annoying bickering going on between two managers. This was the beginning of the end for me.

When I got home I started thinking about the fact I was working long hours, working for somebody else's goals and dreams. My values were now clearly at odds with the company and I decided it was time for me to leave. I thought now it's my time to do something for myself."

Taking the leap of faith

"I discussed everything with my husband, as it is important to gain buy-in from your nearest and dearest. We looked at our finances and saw what kind of cushion we would have if I walked away. I had a week's leave to think everything through and challenge myself. Having made my decision, I wrote my resignation letter. When I went back to work I handed the letter to my boss.

It happened to be the busiest time of the year for the company, so I gave five weeks' notice, a lot more than anybody else would have. As a result, I walked away with my head held high and it was the start of a new and very exciting journey!"

Following my passion

"My passion has always been for writing, I love the written word and I love to read. So the first type of work I started to explore was doing something around writing. Initially I set up as a copywriter. I was writing press releases, articles, newsletters and word copy for small businesses. This business had all been developed as a result of starting to actively network."

The power of networking

"One of the key people who introduced me to networking was a management consultant, who ironically had come to the company just before I left my previous employment. He introduced me to a wonderful lady called Sarah Williams, who is a wordsmith. I went and had a coffee with her and got to know her. Sarah put me in touch with a few local networking groups. I just took that leap of faith and went along because I thought I need to go and meet people, start talking to people. I realised it was the only way people were going to get to know who I am and start

149

this new journey of promoting myself my new business, 'True Expressions'.

I started going to networking events, got to know people and started to build the business. I became a serial networker and built up a lot of my business through face-to-face networking, which I absolutely love. I later decided to write a pocket book on Networking, which I had published."

Evolution

"Between 2005 and 2013, the business was constantly evolving and my portfolio career really developing. During this time, I had trained and qualified as a coach, as a business coach. So I brought business coaching, and also coaching for private clients, into my business. Also, some other strands of my strengths around training and developing people that I really enjoyed from my previous career.

I came to realise that people were 'buying me', Gail Gibson, not my company brand. My business had also changed radically from when I started out, so I rebranded my business to focus on me as the brand and now as a Performance Coach. In doing so, I have brought together my passions for running and the outdoors with coaching, especially women business owners. Therefore, I have I changed the main focus to the key strands of my portfolio career that I enjoy the most and haven't looked back."

What income streams did I let go of in my portfolio and why?

"As I developed and my business grew, changed and morphed into the brand of Gail Gibson today, I decided to let go of those initial strands of copy-writing. It isn't something I am passionate about anymore and I now have a great supply link of people who can do that for me.

However, I still thoroughly enjoy writing my own content. I continue to write copy for just a few long standing clients now, otherwise I forward material to some other people in small businesses who write really well. What it allows me is the **choice to now focus entirely on the things that I really love doing for my clients and offer the things that I am really passionate about in my business.***"*

What is the main strand of my portfolio career that covers most of my bills?

"At the moment it is the business development work with small businesses. I work on a contract basis coaching the senior management team as well as working on business strategy and accountability."

Do I do any voluntary or charity work as part of my portfolio career?

"Back in 2006 I was approached by the editor of our local community magazine to write the business column. The magazine is run by our local churches. I decided to take up the opportunity because I was a new business owner in the local area. I thought it would be a great way to get to know other businesses, to network and to build my business presence. I regularly wrote the business column for a number of years."

What have been my biggest challenges as part of my portfolio career?

"Networking and continuing to network both face to face and online. It's about keeping connections open, revisiting connections and making new connections. Networking has opened so many new doors and opportunities for me. I would say that networking, although a constant challenge, has been instrumental in the success of my portfolio career.

The second key challenge is about resilience. Having a portfolio career, or working for yourself, is about that rollercoaster ride. Those peaks and troughs that you go through. Some are high peaks and when you get to the top and you see the view, it's amazing just to stop think 'I've got through the challenges, I've made things happen and here I am.'

However, things can dip and it can be a short dip or a deep dip. Either way, it's having the right mindset. Being resilient and seeing dips as a new opportunity rather than a threat. Perhaps things haven't worked out, maybe situations where you've come to the end of a journey with somebody or a client. A resilient mindset will allow you to be opportunistic and open new doors so that you can once again ride the upward curve of the rollercoaster.

For me it's been an exciting ride. The challenges have at times caused me to question things or even doubt myself, but ultimately made me stronger, more opportunistic and more positive. As a result, I have grown personally and my business has evolved and thrived."

What have I learnt about working for passion, pleasure and profit?

"I have learnt having a portfolio career is about being open to change. It's about the choices you make and it's been an exciting journey. My business has morphed and changed from being a business offering communications services to now being rebranded as Gail Gibson. I have learnt the importance of honing in on your passions, key skills, talents and key interest areas. These are what ultimately give me the most pleasure and have brought about rewards in terms of increased profits. Underpinning everything is the mix, the variety, which gives me so much pleasure. I really love what I do and the way that I live my

life. The work I do doesn't feel like 'work' because I'm enjoying it so much.

I've actually got to a stage in my business where 80% of my income comes from 20% of my clients, and I can 'play' with the rest of my clients. In particular, I love working on a local basis. Helping my local clients promote and build their businesses is such a great experience."

The importance of Social Media and how it impacts on my portfolio career

"Social media has been something I have taught myself, right from the start of my business and has become a key part of my online networking strategy. Twitter, LinkedIn and Facebook were the platforms I wanted to become part of and know more about. I taught myself how to make effective use of them. As a result, I have become an expert and created new income streams from various coaching programmes, training workshops and Masterclasses. These are mostly to help small businesses make sense of social media and give them the confidence to realise social media isn't the big, scary beast that a lot of people think it is.

I really enjoy using social media to build my brand and online presence. People can get an understanding of who I am, get a feel for my personality and an idea of what my brand is all about. When they meet me in person there really isn't much difference. Social media is a key part of my portfolio career and I really enjoy the mix of it.

Therefore, social media is a continuing part. It's a part of the choice and part of how I deliver my brand. It challenges me and it also allows me to help other businesses, to understand the process and how they can make social media an integrated part of their overall marketing strategy. There isn't digital and traditional media today, it's all about social media as part of your marketing strategy."

If I started my portfolio career again, what would I do differently?

"I often get asked that question and it's like when people say what would you tell your 16-year-old self? Well, I believe that everything that I have done, I've done for a reason and so I wouldn't do anything differently. The people that I have met, the work that I have delivered, the mistakes that I have made and learnt from, and how I've been resilient through the process, it was all part of my life journey and my business and career evolution. So, I would say to people enjoy the adventure and just go with it."

Would I return to a one job employed lifestyle?

"In one word, NO. I now consider myself to be completely unemployable!"

What are the key measures of success in my portfolio career?

"I would say continued belief in myself that I can make this work. I'm someone who is very adventurous in life and I have thoroughly enjoyed the fact that I have fallen into having a portfolio career. I love variety, I love doing different things. I don't think I was ever someone who was meant to have just one role in my life. So it's that self-belief that I can make this work.

Another key measure of success is that I love being opportunistic. I love stepping out there, asking people and getting involved in things. Being opportunistic in approach is the key to the success of any business person today and also a great way to develop collaborations, as I have done with Steve.

It's also about being a leader and leading. Seth Godin, who is a marketing guru I follow, is someone who always talks about being remarkable. Leaders, real leaders, are people who don't follow. I think developing your own brand and developing a successful portfolio career is about you being a leader, how you deliver yourself and what you deliver to people. It's about standing out and being different to other people. So being a strong leader is all about that, being memorable and being remarkable.

The final measure of success is daring, being brave and courageous. It's about facing your fears and letting those fears actually drive you on, which links back to resilience and positive mindset."

Why do I recommend having a portfolio career?

"The word 'choice' is the key to it. Having choice gives you so much variety. When you are working and doing the things that you love, when you are making money from the different parts of your portfolio career, you can have fun, you have a lot of choice and you have diversity. You also have challenge, because you still have that rollercoaster ride, but it's your journey and you will make of it what you will. Having a portfolio career gives you so much more flexibility. For example, you may want to work and travel at the same time. If you want to do a variety of different things, helping different people in different areas, so that you don't have that stagnation of doing the same thing over and over again, as you might in an employed job."

We will revisit Gail's story again in Chapter 6 for a very different lifestyle reinvention of her portfolio career.

Key Learning Points from Gail's story

- Your values are what you hold dear, your authentic self, your code to live by and the foundation on which to build your portfolio career and your happy place

- If you are unhappy in your job or career or with your working lifestyle, assess and challenge your values and needs to help you take the leap of faith and make key changes

- Always be professional to the end and leave your employer on good terms

- Networking is key to developing a successful portfolio career – learn to become a great networker and develop and optimise your networks both online and offline

- Your portfolio will evolve but focus on work you love doing for your clients and are most passionate about in your business – this will then create your pleasure and profit

- Let go of any strands that no longer fit with your values, brand or business goals

- Resilience and a positive mindset are key to your success – ride the rollercoaster and see the dips as an opportunity rather than a threat

- A portfolio career is about choice and embracing change – be brave, face your fears and let your fears drive you on

- Become a leader, be different – develop your own brand and portfolio career

- Social Media is integral to successfully marketing your business – learn to embrace it!

Final Thoughts

It clearly doesn't make sense to continue in any job or career that is making you unhappy. To do so will have a negative domino effect on other aspects of your life and people around you. I have seen so many examples where such frustration and angst reaches boiling point, ready to explode, just like a pressure cooker if no action is taken! Once you establish and become true to your values, you too can be like Gail and find your happy place. Wrestling with them can prolong the process, rather like Julian.

Let's now move onto Chapter 5 and 'Redesign' where you will find out how I met Gail, why we started working together and how our unique approach has inspired many people to shape and create their portfolio careers and working lifestyle approach.

CHAPTER 5

Redesign – Introducing the Portfolio Lifestyle

"Like the sections of a colourful umbrella, you choose from your selection of strengths, skills and talents to best suit you and your clients. Each segment provides you with an opportunity to challenge, to motivate and to grow. With a firm grip on your umbrella, you hold your portfolio life together and it provides a canopy of choice."

Gail Gibson (Business Performance Coach and champion of the portfolio lifestyle)

I have previously defined a 'portfolio career' as a method of deriving income from a number of different sources. It is worth reiterating that it's about changing mindset from having a more conventional job to securing an income by using any combination of activities, interests, skills, talents and passions to create the working lifestyle you want. Furthermore, it is now important to note from the case studies you have read so far, that developing a portfolio career is also a key *lifestyle choice*. In this chapter we will focus on the 'portfolio lifestyle' and take a good look at the associated metaphorical concept of the 'colourful umbrella', i.e. each colourful segment of the open umbrella can represent a different strand of your portfolio. This visual image, along with yet more great case studies, will trigger ideas to help you redesign your own career and working lifestyle too.

What is a Portfolio Lifestyle?

It is about reshaping and redesigning your career and life to generate income in a way that meets all your lifestyle objectives. By focusing on the lifestyle, i.e. a holistic approach, such a perspective will very definitely allow you to take a step aside from conventional, conditioned thinking around the need to have another employed job. Back to that old chestnut again. But now for something completely different!

How Colourful is Your Umbrella?

You have already met Gail in Chapter 4. I first met her online as part of a part of a LinkedIn Portfolio Careers discussion group run by Dr Barrie Hopson (who wrote the foreword to this book). The discussion was around the definition of a portfolio career. Despite having written dozens of business books about careers, portfolio careers and the world of work, Barrie said he had never found a definition of a portfolio career he was really happy with. Enter Gail and the concept of *'the colourful umbrella'*.

It was Gail's fascinating description and metaphor for a portfolio career given above that not only resonated with me, but captivated my attention. It became apparent there were some real synergies between us in the way we shared similar thinking with the group, especially around the portfolio 'lifestyle' aspect. We soon met and a great collaboration and friendship was formed.

The result was developing our *'How Colourful is Your Umbrella – Creating Your Portfolio of Choice'*, Portfolio Career and Lifestyle concept. For a number of years, we developed a range of inspirational seminars and Masterclasses and also published a popular 2 CD/MP3 set audio book. We shared the concept of the colourful umbrella and the doctrine of the portfolio lifestyle at numerous conferences and professional associations. We even ran some highly successful premium executive coaching sessions where the clients had the benefit of both myself and Gail, working in tandem to help them create their 'colourful umbrella' and portfolio of choice.

We had great fun working together and were constantly coming up with new ideas to improve the colourful umbrella concept and marketability. It also was wonderful to see the results of our efforts and helping to inspire a new breed of portfolio careerist to become lifestyle focused. As I mentioned in Chapter 1, not everyone 'got it'. Things evolve, as I have shown consistently in this book. Therefore, it was time for a different approach that would still create intrigue but in a way that was more obvious. As you saw in Chapter 4, Gail has since developed her business and there is yet more to unveil in Chapter 6. This then became an opportune time for me to expand and embellish the portfolio career and lifestyle idea under my brand and the concept of *'Working for Passion, Pleasure and Profit'* and the *3 Ps* were born.

However, I still use the colourful umbrella concept to showcase how you can create a portfolio career of your choice, as it is such a great analogy. It is also such a visually compelling way to show how each segment can represent a different strand of your portfolio. I have recreated a special version of the umbrella specifically for this book, as many of the case studies have inspired me with some new thinking in terms of the holistic working and portfolio lifestyle concept.

The different strands are purely illustrative as they may not all be directly applicable to you – no one size 'fits all' as you can combine and vary the different strands to suit your unique work-life blend and income needs. Unfortunately, the nature of book publication, does not always allow for a true 'colourful' umbrella image. Therefore, to make the same distinction the strands are shaded with patterns to convey the original meaning.

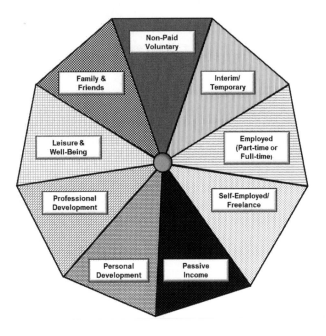

The strands are generally self-explanatory; however, it's important to note that there could also be crossover between some of the strands and that there is no particular order or sequence. So, in no particular order let's take a closer look at these. Where possible I will relate them to case studies featured or other examples for ease of understanding, especially where there might be crossover. Also, whilst it is not my main purpose to recreate the many specific examples of 21st century work options that are featured in Chapter 5 of my *Winning Through Career Change book*, I feel it is beneficial to understand some options that might fall under different strands of the umbrella.

Employed (part-time or full-time)

In Chapter 1 we covered the make -up of a 'typical' portfolio career, which included different variations, including a range of employed part-time jobs and also combining either part-time or full-time jobs with other options. In Chapter 4 Julian's case study is a great example of having a number of different portfolio strands, blending a full time employed job with self-employment and also being a partner in another company. Moreover, Julian has never lost his lifestyle focus with leisure and well-being (especially taking long holidays) his family and friends and both his personal and professional development being important strands of his colourful umbrella.

Regular part-time work

As mentioned, many portfolio careerists have some form of regular employed part-time work. That's relatively straightforward and this is often a lifestyle choice. Moreover, this category is often a good example of where strands can crossover to combine with others and make things even more interesting. For example, my wife is engaged in part-time work for a regular number of days per week on a self-employed 'consultancy' basis. Unlike the employed part-timers where she works, she isn't bound by having to take holidays at specific times or other restrictive terms and conditions. She has a high degree of flexibility and choice but will also cover for other staff as and when she can. She also fits other strands of her portfolio work around these commitments. In my experience, some people value the greater certainty of income derived from regular part-time work. This can instil a confidence that affords the opportunity to develop other stands to your portfolio.

Personal and Professional Development

Both are important considerations within a portfolio career and lifestyle. I am purposefully making the distinction, as my experience is there is often confusion between the two.

Although there can be some crossover, I will simplify to help you when creating your colourful umbrella.

Personal Development

Personal development is also known as self-development or personal growth. Think of personal development like going to the gym. However, instead of developing your muscles, you are developing your mind, e.g. expanding your self-awareness, confidence, self-esteem and improving your personal and life skills. Feza made a number of references to the benefits and importance of ongoing personal development in his case study in Chapter 2. By focusing on personal development you will enhance the quality of your life, contribute to setting and realising of goals, dreams and aspirations, all essential ingredients for creating a successful portfolio career. From my perspective, this also means aspiring to become the best person you can be. For some people this may involve spiritual development too.

Professional Development

In contrast professional development is focused on the learning, obtaining or maintaining of professional credentials or formal qualifications required for your profession, e.g. degrees or vocational qualifications. Continued professional development (CPD) can be achieved through attending and learning from conferences, seminars, workshops and courses related to the job, career or business sector/s you are involved in. In my case, my main professional development in my portfolio career has been related to the training, formal and informal qualifications I have gained as a coach and consultant.

Passive Income

If you were not familiar with this term, Feza's case study in Chapter 2 may have helped you learn about the benefits passive income can bring. Understanding passive income may change your perspective on how you earn, opening up a whole new world of work and lifestyle opportunities. *Why?* Because… passive income is an income received on a regular basis, often with little effort required to maintain it. Typical examples could be:

- Earnings from a business that does not require your direct involvement as the owner

- Any type of property income, including rental/buy to let

- Dividends and interest from stocks and shares and financial investments

- Earnings from network marketing/multi-level marketing* activities from your team

- Royalties from publishing a book or music, licensing a patent or other form of intellectual property, such as computer software product

- Earnings from internet advertisements on websites or affiliate marketing

- Earnings from products you have created, e.g. audio books, online programmes and webinars

- Building online businesses that take advantage of automated systems to enable transactions, cash flow and growth to happen without requiring a real-time presence

You will see many examples of people and organisations who glorify passive income as *'earning money while you are lying on a beach or when you are sleeping'*. Such marketing unfortunately gives a false impression. Therefore, many people think that passive income is about getting something for nothing, as it has a 'get rich quick' appeal. The reality, as proven by Feza in Chapter 2, is that the benefit from passive income still requires hard work or some form of financial investment. The difference is you do the hard work upfront and then reap the reward later. Don't be misled in this respect. Feza's case study also highlighted the value of network marketing. Although this approach has made many millionaires and can be a great lifestyle choice, it's not for everyone.

My passive income is derived from many sources, e.g. royalties on my books, audio books and online career development programmes. We have also seen a number of examples throughout the book where people are deriving regular passive income from property rentals.

Self-employed/freelance

'Self-employed' is the term used to describe someone working for themselves, either in a freelance capacity or as an owner of a business. In effect you are working for yourself independently and not for any other company. **You therefore earn your living by selling your services or products to other companies/organisations or maybe even individual private clients.**

The term 'freelancing' is most common in culture and creative industries. For instance, although our son is self-employed and has a business trading name, he markets himself as a 'freelance sound engineer', as this is what is expected in his industry.

Instead of being totally reliant on marketing yourself or your business, another option is for you to work for an established business, which uses a team of associates in your field of specialism, e.g. Coaching. This is exactly what my company does. As my company has grown over the years, I have continually added to my associate team for specialist projects, e.g. Outplacement, Executive, Management and Team Coaching and Development.

When I started out as self-employed, in addition to marketing and delivering projects for my own business, I was an associate for a training company and have also been an associate for a few HR and Career Management Consultancies. The benefits are that you do not have to look for the business but the downside is that you are unlikely to be able to negotiate your fees, as these will usually be set by the company. Being an associate is also a good option as part of a portfolio career as you can then develop other strands alongside this you market under your own brand.

Interim Management

Interim Management is becoming increasingly important in the business mix; a much more hands on alternative to Management Consultancy. Providing the temporary provision of management resources and skills, Interim Management can be seen as the short term assignment to manage a period of transition, crisis or change within an organisation. In such situations a permanent candidate may be unnecessary, or impossible to find at short notice, as there may be a skills or availability shortage within the organisation.

Across all sectors, tens of thousands of interims are employed to cover unexpected gaps, deliver key projects, or drive change and growth. Interims are seen as a source of competitive advantage which is the best description of the way they are used in today's market.

Interim Management is difficult to get into but once you develop a reputation you can be in constant demand and make a great living. Interim Management is definitely an option to sit within a portfolio career. Some people look at the interim route for the lifestyle benefits of not having a permanent role and the flexibility and freedom this offers. Many interims have multiple income streams, as they either don't want to be always delivering or chasing new interim assignments or they enjoy the variety of doing other work in between interim assignments. I also know interims who work on highly paid projects for a few months before taking time out to travel, or engage with other lifestyle projects, before seeking their next interim role. Others prefer to constantly be working on projects. As always, you have **choice!**

What is the difference between an interim and a temp or contractor?

An important distinction to make is the difference between the temp/contract market and genuine interim roles. While temporary roles are typically tactical (maintaining steady state), interim roles require genuine change agents who can demonstrate knowledge transfer, legacy creation and a consistently compelling return on investment. There is some crossover. Some sectors, notably IT, have a preference towards 'contractors', whilst Finance, Marketing, HR and Operations tend to recruit for interim roles at manager or director level.

Family and friends

Not everyone will want to focus on spending more time with family and friends. However, you will have seen a number of references throughout the book where I have stated this is a key lifestyle objective many people tell me they want to achieve. Although it may be implied in some of the case studies, it is particularly relevant to Jane's case study in Chapter 3, and even more so in Part 2 of her story that follows below. Valuing your family and friends can become especially important when looking to make key changes in your life, such as developing a portfolio career. Having such a support mechanism and getting them on board with your ideas is invaluable, just as my best friend Don and I did for each other during our respective career transitions.

When coaching clients, I am often saddened and horrified when I hear statements such as 'I have lost touch with most of my friends' or 'I rarely get to see my friends as I am always working'. Build it into your umbrella if you want to ensure this is a lifestyle objective.

Leisure and well-being

'Fit in body, fit in mind', as the saying goes. It is well known that physical exercise creates endorphins that improve your well-being and physical stamina. Yet so many people ignore this key aspect of their lifestyle. You can build this into your umbrella and commit to making the change from now.

I have previously shared how I have significantly changed my working lifestyle after re-evaluating my values and needs following my hip replacement. Making time for daily walks, cycling, tennis and body balance classes at the gym are very much part and parcel of my blended portfolio lifestyle. Additionally, there is my love of live music plus making time for regular guitar lessons and practice. We have also seen in Chapter 4 how Gail Gibson has now combined her passion for running, the outdoors and well-being with her love of coaching to successfully rebrand and evolve her portfolio career and lifestyle. Change your mindset and working lifestyle by freeing up time for leisure and well-being activities. They will likely re-energise you and aid your creativity and productivity.

Let's now revisit Marc Blake-Will featured in Chapter 3. In addition to Marc's interesting work portfolio, especially as a comedy writer, he is also a triathlete. Therefore, freeing up the time for his rigorous training schedule is an integral part of his blended portfolio lifestyle. Interestingly, when I interviewed Marc he freely admitted to one of his biggest challenges. **It is the same challenge and 'curse' that also consumes far too many portfolio careerists, myself included for many years. What is it?... It is overcoming 'the guilt factor'.** What do I mean by this? Quite simply *giving yourself permission* to *have flexibility and freedom of choice in the way you work and when you work*. Marc explains:

"I'll find myself wandering off somewhere with a notebook and thinking, do I really deserve this downtime and leisure time because I have chosen a particular portfolio career and lifestyle.

It's like I don't know whether I should be feeling guilty or not, but for some reason I often do. I'm sure people think I'm really lucky as they have to be at work at a given time or work set hours and set days. Then they see me working when I want and going swimming and training for triathlon events during the day. The flip side is I could wake up on a Saturday morning thinking I should be doing some work. Even though I love what I do, I still think I should be doing that. It is crazy really as I could wake up on a Sunday and feel in creative flow and spend the day writing, when other people are out enjoying themselves. Even after all these years of having a portfolio career I've got to overcome that obstacle of lifestyle guilt"

Non-paid voluntary

There are many great examples in the book of people who devote a regular part of their working week or time periodically to some form of voluntary work. Essentially this is all about performing or providing a service willingly and without pay. This can be quite an altruistic activity as it fulfils the human need or desire to selflessly help others.

I have mentioned that aside of my keynote and well paid private sector speaking engagements, I often give my time for free to speak at business libraries, professional associations and executive job clubs. I have clients who are trustees for charities and school governors. These are significant roles but non-paid, except for maybe out of pocket expenses. Many such roles were previously thought of the domain for the 'retired' or semi-retired. However, my experience is that people often undertake all sorts of voluntary roles to benefit a cause they are passionate about, for a new challenge and often to develop new skills that could be valuable in other aspects of strands in a portfolio career.

For anyone looking to change career or transform their working lifestyle, doing some form of voluntary work can prove to be an enormous benefit. In the process you are likely to meet new people, develop new networks and it could spark a new lease of life, just as it did with my wife.

Crossover – Non-Executive Directors (NEDs)

I wish to reiterate the importance of 'crossover' between the various strands of the umbrella and how many can co-exist to provide you with a rich and diverse portfolio career. I am highlighting NED roles, as depending on your business and professional career background, NED roles could be of interest as they sit well within a portfolio career as we will see shortly with the next case study and also Carol in Chapter 6.

NEDs are prevalent in the private, public and not-for-profit sectors and are usually retained for a particular number of days per month. The principal role of a non-executive director is that of 'critical friend' to the organisation. This is someone who not only supports the executive directors and can act as an ambassador, but is also able to view the Board objectively and challenge the organisational strategy. The crossover is that NEDs are either non-paid voluntary roles whilst others are fee paying roles, so could sit in different strands of your umbrella. There are all sorts of complex rules and tax implications for NEDs, which may also vary between countries. Always best to thoroughly research such roles first, if of interest. For many people such roles really provide an opportunity to make a difference.

Why become a Non-Executive Director?

People become Non-Executive Directors for various reasons:

1. As part of a Portfolio Career, where they will have a number of part-time remunerated roles often combined with interim, consultancy, coaching and mentoring work

2. In order to develop their Boardroom skills either in conjunction with, or preparation for, an executive role

3. As a way of 'giving something back'. Increasingly non-executive, trustee or governor roles (with a social

enterprise) or other not-for-profit organisations, are seen as more effective ways of volunteering than high street fundraising or sponsored activities

4. To 'keep your hand in' after you have stepped down from a senior executive role in a major corporate, large public or not-for-profit sector organisation

5. To be part of the excitement of the next generation of entrepreneurs on the Board of a start-up or high growth business

Similar to Interim Management, it can be challenging to secure NED roles but once you do and develop a reputation, this then puts you in good stead for future opportunities.

📖 Case Study: David's Story

Non Executive Director and Multiple Business Owner

"Life isn't very long; you only get one shot at it. To me, it seems a waste to spend five days a week earning enough money to do what you really wanted to do at the weekend. Sadly, this seems to be the way a lot of people view their careers."

Meet David Doughty, another fascinating character. His portfolio career is very different to the majority of people I know because he runs multiple businesses all set up as separate limited companies! This isn't my idea of a 'simple' and 'fun' portfolio career, but David seems to thrive on it. Yet more proof there isn't a one size fits all approach to developing a portfolio career **as it all comes back to choice.**

My Portfolio

"I chair a health quango, I chair a charity, again involved in health. I have quite an interest in the NHS, in health. I'm

a non-exec director on a global investment fund coming from India but based in Luxembourg. I'm on the advisory Board of a global recruitment company that does Board-level recruitment. I also run my own businesses which are in Board development, corporate governance, non-executive development and executive coaching based on career transitions. This is particularly focused on people who are moving out of a corporate career into a portfolio career."

How did my portfolio career develop?

"I don't think there was one thing. It was a gradual process. It started off naturally, but it has evolved. Often, when you start up on your own, (you see it a lot with people, especially if they've had a corporate life), you might start off as John Smith Limited or John Smith Associates. You try and do different things through one company, one brand. However, I think other people find that hard to understand. So I deliberately set up differently. I'm now managing about eighteen different brands through eight limited companies.

I got my first non-exec position about 12 years ago. I suppose before then, I never really had a traditional career anyway because it had been a mixture of starting my own businesses. I was a serial entrepreneur but also in between times, either being a consultant or actually being an employee of other organisations. So already, I had a mixture of different roles and was arguably developing my portfolio career, even then.

I never really did more than one thing at a time until about 12 years ago when I started doing non-exec roles as well as a full-time career. But again, that full-time career was as a founder of my own business. I sold that business in 2007, then I became much more of a portfolio careerist.

Although I did go into full-time employment after that, I had a number of non-exec positions at the same time. Then when that full-time employed role finished, towards the end of 2010, I've been pretty much full-time as a portfolio careerist. Non-exec roles in private, public and voluntary sectors, consultancy and starting my own businesses at the same time. So, those are the three strands of what I'm doing at the moment."

Why did I set up as so many different companies?

"For me that was a deliberate decision to take. Having been involved in helping other people trying to unravel and unwind bits of businesses because somebody wanted to buy a piece of it but not all of it, I thought, I might as well start from scratch and each separate strand would be a limited company.

My business set up makes it a much easier and neater way to own Intellectual Property for example. It also means people have the opportunity to buy one part of my business, rather than having to buy all of it, which they might not be interested in."

Do I have a main business strand?

"The one main strand is the Board development, non-executive director development roles. So, that's the main stream in terms of what I call my 'day job', which involves corporate governance. But even that business consists of consultancy, training, development and coaching. So, even that's a multiple strand too!"

What has been my biggest challenge?

"You might think it would be starting up multiple businesses. However, having had a career that involves start-up businesses, having started one business,

starting up eight businesses at the same time was not a particular challenge, because it's something that I'm very much used to.

Marketing is the number one challenge. *I am consciously developing a multiple approach to marketing. Getting the message across and with clarity, so people know what it is that you're offering. So, positioning in the market, making clear offerings to people is the biggest challenge.*

A benefit of having the luxury of multiple businesses and brands means you can focus on the one that's proving to be the most interesting and that gets the best reception from people, whilst you're developing the others. So, you're not just relying on one particular strand or one particular brand to see you through.

I think the other thing is when you start a business, quite often there's a lot of things that don't happen. You put yourself out in the market, send out a lot of information and then you wait for something to happen. You are also out there, busy networking. So, it takes a while for the business to start coming in. I find if you're doing that in multiple dimensions, you can actually manage your time much better. It's the sort of epiphany of exactly what it is that you have to offer. So although to the outside world it seems as if I'm doing a lot of different things, in my mind it's just me and it's commercialising what I've got to offer."

What have I learnt along the way?

"I think my main learning was exactly what I did have to offer. It's the transition from making a living out of what I can do and what I can deliver, to what I know. It's selling the knowledge that I've got and matching that knowledge

with what people actually want to buy. That knowledge of how to do things that work for you and your clients.

Also, a portfolio career is different and it's not for everyone. Some people like the stability of one job, doing one thing and the 9-to-5. But for me it's the fact that with the variety of what I do, it doesn't seem like work. I love what I do and it's a way of life."

What do I enjoy most about having a portfolio career?

"To me, a portfolio career it's about living and breathing. Being a bit selfish I suppose. Doing what you want to do on your terms and enjoying it. Equally, having the ability to walk away from things you're not particularly enjoying.

I think one of the great attractions is there's never two days the same. I really enjoy getting a couple of empty days in the diary when I can think and develop and do some marketing. However, it's rare to get that because it's usually a lot going on but there are a lot of variations in that.

I also think part of the self-realisation is that I am actually now unemployable!

In summary, life isn't very long and you only get one shot at it. To me, it seems a waste to spend five days a week earning enough money to do what you really wanted to do at the weekend. Sadly, this seems to be the way a lot of people view their careers."

Key Learning Points from David's story

- Running multiple businesses might not be the ideal for all portfolio careerists, but David has proven that this set up can be pleasurable and profitable

- Depending on your career and business background, Non-Executive Director (NED) roles can be a great option and addition to a portfolio career

- You can be 'jack of all trades and master of many' – positioning is key so match your knowledge with what people want to buy

- Marketing and clarity of your offering/s is often the biggest challenge for portfolio careerists

- If you have multiple businesses, or business strands, you can focus on one strand or business that is getting the most interest whilst you are developing the others

- It's helpful to get some free time for thinking and developing your portfolio/business

- Having a portfolio career is not just about the work you do it is a way of life

Creating your own colourful umbrella

Now you have seen examples of how you can create a colourful umbrella to combine a portfolio career with your lifestyle of choice. So how can you now replicate the process to create your own? What aspects would you build into the different strands of your umbrella? This is not an easy exercise and something that forms a key part of my <u>Portfolio Career Masterclasses</u> and coaching sessions. To help you get started here are 4 key questions that have helped unlock new thinking for many clients:

Q1. Imagine you are now a portfolio careerist – what would your ideal day or week look like?

What activities? Where? With whom? What experiences would you like to be in your ideal week?

Q2. What work/activities would you like to be doing if everything paid the same?

Really think broadly and consider your passions, interests, hobbies and things you may have often thought about in the past but dismissed

Q3. What work/activities do you enjoy or would like to try but not on a full-time basis?

This could include ideas for a home based business, creative work, projects, volunteering etc.

Q4. What problems can you solve that other people will pay for?

You will need to make a living from your portfolio career to achieve the working lifestyle you desire. So consider your range of skills and talents and how you could use some of these to earn income in different ways?

Not easy is it? You might find reflecting on these questions will help. Often your unconscious mind will kick into play and you could wake up one morning with your head brimming full of great ideas!

Let's now revisit Steve, who we met in Chapter 3, to learn more about how he developed his colourful umbrella and the amazing transformation that took place in his life.

📖 *Case Study: Steve's Story (Part 2)*

This remarkable thing called NLP!

"There were a number of us in the room, some great people, doing a series of exercises. It was Steve and Gail's 'How Colourful is Your Umbrella' Portfolio Career Masterclass. We had a bunch of cards, all sorts of papers, coloured pens and goodness knows what else. The real challenge was this thing called a 'portfolio career', which I hadn't really known of in my working career. I began to discover what it really meant. What unlocked it again for me was the power of the metaphor, 'the colorful umbrella', the colourful strands, each representing a particular potential income stream, a contribution in some way to a portfolio career.

We were asked to map out and consider the component strands of our umbrella. I began with the new strands that I'd come to know, such as the PowerPoint presentations. Then I remember penciling it in, three letters on one of the strands of the umbrella. I remember gazing at the three letters and I couldn't hear anything else in the room, thinking, wondering if I could do this. These were the letters NLP... Neuro Linguistic Programming. It was something that had intrigued me for a number of years but I had never had the time to properly research. Basically NLP brings together the dynamics of our mind, together with the language we use and how the two interplay... just like a computer programme."

Strange things happening all over again

"You make all these positive connections/intentions and then there seems to be something interwoven in some way in the fabric of the universe that can make it happen. Coincidentally, (or was it?), Steve Preston had previously done some basic NLP training and gave me a recommendation. I investigated and researched it online and the recommendation looked to be the most intriguing. This company seemed to offer the best training and also best value for money.

Unfortunately, I had just missed NLP Level One training and so went straight into the more advanced Practitioner training programme. There were some gaps, but this didn't seem to concern the Master NLP trainer delivering it... even that started to intrigue me. There's no doubt about it. This wasn't what I remember to be training. It wasn't a chore; it wasn't hard work. This was something quite different, this was something I enjoyed doing and I thought, 'What would it be like if I could actually do some NLP for a living and earn some income as part of a portfolio career?' Doing something, I know and love and get paid for it, I thought, 'This is unheard of!'

I completed the training and all the assessments in record time, including backtracking to retrospectively complete Level One. I thought 'I can't stop here, this is too much fun' and then decided to continue with the NLP Master Practitioner Level. This is where you put aside the theory and really start to understand and achieve mastery in the subject... a real challenge.

*However, much to my delight I soon completed a comprehensive NLP modelling project and qualified as an NLP Master Practitioner. **This then continued the theme, this pattern, this trend of doing something*** *positive and it leading to something else... but doing something you really enjoy."*

The power of feedback works again

"During the training I would occasionally offer general comments on the NLP training material and manuals. I would casually point out to the MD of the company any spelling mistakes and where some parts of the text/ content didn't quite make sense. This, coupled with such a detailed submission for my modelling project, allowed the MD to realise I had quite an eye for detail and so he was happy to make any corrections. He then asked for my input on the design of some pop-up display banners. To my amazement he took the comments on board and made the changes. This then lead to a few other things I didn't expect. The MD writes regular articles to publish and asked me if I would proof-check them. At this point, as with the presentations and other work I had done for Steve, the issue of payment was mentioned. Having worked in the public sector for almost 40 years with a guaranteed income each month, this was totally new territory for me. So this really was the birth, this new renaissance, of my portfolio career and lifestyle.

The nature of the work went beyond proof-checking and I now this to be content editing and developing. I actually re-wrote some of his articles in the greater part, as I struggled with some of the terminology, the words, the sentence construction, grammar. The MD took it all in good stead and we developed a very strong rapport and a great level of trust. I then learnt he was dyslexic, which made some of his written issues more understandable. However, it amazed me how much effort he had gone to overcome his dyslexia. NLP itself was a particular method and technique. He has also transformed his shyness to become an outstanding and well respected NLP Master-

Trainer and Master Practitioner. So I had nothing but admiration for him and I was very keen to help him all the more.

He then asked me to write some challenging reports on various coaching topics. I was initially at a loss as to why he was asking me to write about 'coaching', as I hadn't considered myself as a coach. It was only when I questioned this with different people, they made me realise I had actually been coaching for years in my previous management career. My natural coaching style had created a positive impact on people and NLP colleagues had described me as having an effective 'quiet charisma' that quickly yielded trust. The MD loved the completed reports and this was more paid-for work. This evolved into becoming a guest blogger on the company website, which I readily accepted.

Around this time, the MD was being sidelined by a huge project, where he was personally delivering all the training, as well as doing everything else. He remarked some things were suffering. So I took on other activities to relieve the pressure on him. Then the real 'golden nugget'... 'By the way, I am rewriting and rebuilding the hypnosis training from the ground up, and I wonder whether you might like to help deliver it?'

That blew me away because hypnosis has been one of my passions within NLP as I seemed to have the most profound transformational effects very quickly and unexpectedly. So I'm now looking to train more and gain further accreditation in Hypnosis with a view to helping to deliver future training programmes. I am so grateful to this exceptional NLP company for such wonderful feedback and new opportunities."

How has my portfolio career evolved?

"It's literally a repeat of this strange phenomenon, process, of doing one thing and it leading to another. Also, a growing realisation of your value, your work, which leads in itself to bringing back the confidence that I probably lost in my previous employed role in local government.

To be surrounded by nothing but positive people breeds that positive mindset in yourself. So it wasn't a conscious decision. But by trying new things, where my talents were openly valued and acknowledged with positive feedback, the more I wanted to give."

What have been my biggest challenges?

"Transitioning from a lengthy public sector role at my time of life and letting go of my HR past. Then accepting I am really being valued for my work and even more so, accepting I am actually getting paid my true worth for it!

I was also always looking for feedback, positive feedback. However, that feedback has gradually transformed into a tangible income. **My biggest challenge, since accepting I am genuinely being valued for the work I do, has been to ensure I get paid 'my true worth'."**

What does success mean for me?

"For me it's never really been about the money itself. Maybe you've earned X amount on one day or for a project. The money represents something else for me and it goes back to value and being valued. UK business guru, Peter Thomson says, "Money is the silent applause for a job well done". This has always stuck with me. Even though it's not about the money, it has taken me a few years to come to terms with that fact that people were

taking advantage of my initial business naivety and giving nature. I always want recognition, always have done, always will do. Recognition is now coming in the form of payment; profit for work that gives me pleasure."

Would I go back to another employed job?

"It's funny I've had this conversation with my wife a couple of times. When I see what she's doing I have said to her, 'I couldn't go back doing that.' I think it's just so constraining and so restrictive in terms of creativity. So, no I would not and could not go back to typical employed life, with the realisation there are things out there that give much more enjoyment in life."

Would I recommend the portfolio career working lifestyle?

"Absolutely! It's an opportunity to do one of a number of things at any one time. You can keep your options open, not to be restricted, not to be constrained, to dip-in and dip-out of different things. One thing I haven't said is about the benefit of meeting so many different people. I think the people have been a significant part of my transition; very influential and I use the term 'lucky'. Although, I'm questioning myself, as meeting such different people, perhaps that wasn't luck. It was just the fact that I 'chose' this route and then made an effort to meet people that created these continuous avenues. One thing I do know for sure from my NLP training... there will be no improvement, change or transformation without the commitment to take action... and that's the difference between success and failure.

In summary the portfolio career represents variety, a wide range of opportunities that are of benefit to you as a person as well as other people... so it's a 'win-win' *situation.* **Why be constrained and restricted in doing one thing, in a corporate world for example, when you could do any number of things that you love and enjoy and are passionate about as part of a portfolio career?**

As a result of my journey, NLP has helped to transform my life and that of others. You can't ask for better than this!"

Key Learning Points from Steve's story (Part 2)

- If you have an interest in something that creates intrigue, follow your instinct and explore it as you never know where it might lead

- Age is just a state of mind – you are never too old to develop new skills and passions

- Developing your portfolio career with totally new income streams will also re-energise you

- Even if money isn't your main driver, from a business and professional perspective, understand and ensure you receive your true worth as recognition for the value you add

- Go out and meet new and different types of people as you never know where it will lead you

- Positive people help to breed a positive mindset making you want to give and excel more

- A portfolio career is worlds apart from an institutionalised public sector or corporate life

- You have no need to ever feel constrained – keep your options open instead

Downsize Your Career, Upsize Your Life

This is another perspective and way to 'frame' the portfolio lifestyle. I wrote some articles about this topic of downsizing your career and upsizing your life a few years ago. They attracted much interest, attention and mainly positive comment, which suggested to me I had hit on a nerve! As with the colourful umbrella concept, you can't appeal to everyone as there were some inevitable concerns about the perceptions of 'downsizing your career'. Some felt this would devalue what they do.

The reality of what's happening in the current world of work

In Chapter 2 we explored the changing world of work and impact of the changing demographics. Like it or not, we are constantly bombarded with headlines about the impact of volatile stock markets, currency markets, public sector cutbacks, corporate reorganisation, job losses and the fact that the age to collect a pension for many people has advanced beyond 65 years. What does this illustrate? It paints a picture of lack of job security and the benefit of taking control of your own career and life to fit into these changing times.

Becoming more apparent is a change in thinking

In Chapter 2 I also mentioned there is a 'revolution' happening in the world of work around us. More and more people are starting to see the impact of the changing face of work in their own lives. As a result, growing numbers of people have chosen to make time to *create their own work and life'*, hence the explosion in self-employed/freelancers. For many the time has come to bring about a better **blend** of 'work' and 'life', to realise a dream, to spend quality time with loved ones or to pursue an interest or passion. People, like Steve, are standing up and saying, *"No longer will I be held back by the constraints of having a job when I can create a bespoke working lifestyle"*. The portfolio career has now become an accepted and alternative way of earning a living – even more so when focused on the portfolio lifestyle.

Is now the time for you to consider 'downsizing' your career to upsize your life?

You might feel you cannot see how you can downsize your career due to financial and personal responsibilities such as mortgage, family commitments and living expenses. However, consider your career – where are you at right now, what do you aspire to achieve, and where do you see your current work taking you?

Next, challenge yourself to review any career related issues you may have. Are you stressed, do you work long hours, how much time do you spend with your family and friends, how much time do you get to do the things you love or are you experiencing problems at home?

Does your career provide you with a healthy, happy and fulfilling lifestyle where you enjoy what you do and you can spend quality time with your loved ones? Typically, a review will highlight key positive and negative aspects of your career. It may even unearth a previously unseen realisation or light bulb moment which presents an opportunity to perhaps adopt a Portfolio Lifestyle.

Take a more in depth approach to your review and, like we saw with Gail in Chapter 4, ask yourself *"Is my vision blurred because I am so busy working toward someone else's goals and dreams that I have in fact lost sight of my own life?"* In reply to your answer you can then ask yourself, *"Is my challenge to step out of someone else's life and step into and really live my own life?"* It's advisable to conduct a thorough review of your finances to be clear that you have sufficient household income to meet your commitments. It's wise to take into account personal savings as well as any income from your partner, siblings, dividends and investments etc. Chances are the reality will hit home and the prospect of developing a portfolio lifestyle will become even more attractive. In my experience, if you want to make it work you will, providing you have the confidence, self-belief and are prepared take positive action.

How can a Portfolio Lifestyle work?

A successful portfolio life is a curious and self-fulfilling mix of challenge, diversity and inspiration. This alternative way of thinking, working and living provides you with an opportunity to embrace choice, freedom and purpose. Perhaps the greatest aspect of this working lifestyle is that you can choose who you work with, how you work with them, when you work and where you work. It's all about **choice, your choice.**

Back in Chapter 2 I challenged conventional work patterns. There is no rule that states you must work a typical Monday to Friday 5-day week. By adopting a portfolio lifestyle, you can work in the best way to suit your personal situation, your clients or customers and the type of work you do. For example, Gail Gibson's husband works for the RAF. Over many years Gail has become accustomed to him going on tours of duty and also numerous weekend training courses and events. As a result, she has adapted her working lifestyle to ensure they spend quality time together whenever he is home. His schedule means this could often be during the week and not at weekends. Consequently, Gail will maximise her working time when he is away and is often happy to work Sundays. This makes perfect sense and comes back to your **choice** in your working lifestyle **blend**.

I remember many years ago being surprised but most impressed, by an Interim HR Director who had split their typical working week. She worked in corporate HR from Monday to Thursday and then as a school teacher on the remaining Friday. She was not contactable on Fridays by her HR colleagues and made it quite clear that nothing would interfere or disrupt her passion and love for teaching; a commitment made to a close friend. This was very definitely a 'win-win' situation where she could combine all her interests as part of her portfolio career. She resolutely stuck to this working pattern and negotiations for any other interim roles offered had to fit with her working lifestyle choice.

You could argue that taking such an approach would restrict opportunities to secure good Interim HR roles. However, as demonstrated throughout this book, if your contribution is truly valued then you have the power to negotiate and influence contracts or projects on your terms. A particularly good example of this follows with the continuation of Jane's story.

📖 *Case Study: Jane's Story (Part 2)*

Planning the next phase of life

Let's now revisit Jane who we met in Chapter 3. Since her original interview with me Jane has turned fifty and has decided it is time to redesign her career and life. She has taken the learning from Chapter 4, in terms of *rediscover*, and combined this with portfolio lifestyle concept of this chapter.

By working hard, building up a good 'war chest', re-evaluating their values and finances, Jane and her husband have taken a huge leap of faith. They have started on the next phase of their lives and adopted a very different 'portfolio lifestyle' approach, which is set to transform their future.

Having initially invested in a property in Spain a few years ago, Jane and her husband's dream was of eventually spending their retirement between the UK and Spain. However, Jane decided a change of plan was required to bring forward their 'retirement'. Having now sold their family home and even Jane's beloved car, they have downsized both their house and cars to be mortgage free. They have purchased a smaller house that has great rental potential for future passive and Jane now shares a car with her husband. The resulting released equity has enabled them to design and build a beautiful state-of-the-art luxury wide beam narrowboat. They are now realising their dream of living afloat, minimising living costs, exploring the waterways and facilitating a healthier lifestyle. Jane's redesigned portfolio lifestyle is now a great blend of working when, where and how much she chooses, cruising on the waterways or relaxing at their Spanish home.

'Dunstressin'

Jane's husband has taken early retirement and project managed their house move and boat build. Having introduced Jane to Tara Winona (see her case study Chapter 2), Jane has also become a huge fan of her amazing art. They have agreed on an exciting plan for Tara to paint a very special tree of life (one of her signature creations) as a mural on the side of the boat. This will be a wonderful addition to Tara's portfolio career and I'm sure a fabulous creation for Jane's canal cruiser.

They even have an idea for using their boat for a special art tour, with Tara, to have a mobile gallery for her work in different parts of the UK. Jane's husband has also taken up photography and is keen to further develop this passion, which will be a great way to showcase their ever-changing new lifestyle on the canals in the UK and potentially Europe.

Jane has always been involved in various aspects of voluntary work; an important part of who she is and her desire to give back to the community. She is looking at involvement with the Canal and River Trust, which may even provide the opportunity for some foster caring.

Jane has also changed her business model and now chooses to work only three days a week. Instead of delivering the majority of the projects herself, she has changed her business set up to enable her to more easily subcontract work to trusted contacts and ex-colleagues. This approach has been a huge mindset shift for Jane, rather than doing the majority of work herself. Jane will become a 'Digi nomad' as outlined in Chapter 2. She will also very selectively choose the projects and clients she wants to work with. This way Jane will have the freedom to work remotely from their cruiser, their Spanish home or work on site and live away for periods of time.

This whole project and change process has enabled Jane and her husband to be financially self-sufficient and mortgage free. Their new life plan is to ideally spend their winters and spring in their Spanish home and summer and autumn in the UK. They will be truly the living the dream and living even more so by Jane's values and on her terms. *"What's the name of the boat?"* I hear you say. Well, in recognition of what they are looking to achieve in their lives moving forward, it is poignantly called *'Dunstressin'*. What a great story, case study and inspirational twist in her next phase of life! You can now read Jane's summary of her portfolio career journey and evolution.

What have been my key challenges and learning points?

"I guess the key one is financially; actually understanding cash flow and running a business or setting up as a business, understanding all of the aspects of running a limited company. Also, on the cash flow side, the golden rule for me is to remember to factor in that it could take up to three months to win a contract. Therefore, I still need to forward plan, but not put all my eggs in one

basket and consider earning opportunities across all of my portfolio revenue generating strands.

A big challenge, and it was a personal challenge for me is, is that I tend to be a perfectionist. You therefore need to learn when 'good' is 'good enough' because it is easy to get too involved, go too deep when it isn't needed. Also, when it's somebody's else's money you have to balance that, as time is money.

One key thing you taught me, Steve, is to create your own support network through your own network. So, if I'm not sure about something, I can phone or email someone and they will usually answer and help me with my query or we can bounce ideas around to mutual benefit.

One of the things I am now very clear about is only taking on projects I want to take and only on my terms. An example is negotiating to engage an assignment where I was determined to only work either two or three days a week. This is my choice, because I want to have more work across the range of my portfolio rather than have too much work of just one strand.

I have another home in Spain, so I value having flexibility. Also, a few years ago, when my father was ill, I was able to be with him and take him to hospital when he needed. This is time that I would never have had if I stayed in my corporate role.

I was engaged with a client at the time but reduced my available days to work around the appointments. The client still had the same deliverables but was understanding and prepared to work around my revised working model as I had the skillset they needed. The flexibility worked in their favour by spreading the cost and for me with a slightly longer engagement, but on my terms. <u>What I learnt is if a client really wants you and</u> <u>they are buying you for your skills and expertise, you can</u> <u>use your influence to manage the contract around your</u> <u>situation and availability.</u> Therefore, they'll usually work to your terms. If not, then it's not the contract for me, or I will find other associates to cover the rest of the week for me so it's a 'win-win' on both fronts."

Collaborations

"I have come to realise teaming up with other people is very important, as the sum of the whole is greater than the parts. Depending on the nature of your work, you should not try to do everything yourself. However, collaborations need more thought than I expected. Although everybody has their own values, you need to make sure the people you collaborate with have the same underpinning values. For example, I've got a very strong work ethic. I will always work to get the job done regardless. What I have learnt is, not everybody has that same attitude when they are an independent consultant. Therefore, it's important to bring in the right people for the right project, who will deliver the right result for the client, as it's my business reputation on the line.

Getting the right people for projects will become increasingly important as I take a step back and outsource more work to known, trusted and valued associates under the umbrella of my company. It's great fun to have some of my old team working alongside me, which also provides some breathing space for me."

What would I do differently If I started over again with my portfolio career?

"I would jump in much quicker. It took me ages to get off the ground because I thought I had to have all the 'materials' before I even engaged in a contract. I thought I needed letterheads, compliment slips, all of my frameworks documented, all of my methodologies documented with my logo. I was busy beavering away creating all of these materials only to use about 10% of them! Make sure you plan thoroughly and although you do need a tool-kit most of it is in your head already. You can over-complicate things, you can over-prepare and it's just about, trusting yourself more and going with the flow and just do it."

What do I enjoy most about having a portfolio career?

"I like the flexibility. I've been engaged for fairly long spells with some clients, which has taken me away from home. This is fine but typically I've learnt to not live in hotels, unlike when I was in the corporate world. I like to find an apartment, so my husband or kids could come and visit me, so you make it work for you. What I've done is to negotiate lots of Mondays or Fridays off in return for working full weeks here and there. So, I've typically had 10 weeks' holiday and you certainly can't do that with an employer.

Not only have I worked, but I've actually had the benefit of living in different places throughout the UK. I've lived in Durham, a beautiful City, and was able to explore the Northeast of England from there, staying at weekends and having family come to visit. I've also worked and lived near Bath and other places in the UK I would most likely have never visited.

Many of my assignments have been working in London. I've done this before it's always exciting. It makes a big difference knowing my dreadful commute is only for the duration of the contract, rather than every day. Also, making the most of being in London, spending a *few months of doing things like theatres after work is brilliant. I've also travelled to America, Canada and the Far East. Moreover, there is a big difference working for yourself, as you can build your holidays and flexible days off to actually properly visit the countries. In the corporate world when you travel over a weekend, you tend to work and then it's back-to-back meetings. So, being able to set your own pace and agenda means travel is a luxury and a pleasure, rather than a chore."*

What is success for me?

"The main thing is about ensuring I have a good work-life balance or what I know Steve calls 'blend'. This means different things to different people but my work-life blend enables me to have a certain lifestyle which is quite nice financially. Sometimes I have to stop and pat myself on the back because I have already achieved more than many people achieve in their whole career. I guess success is also confidence for me and re-engagement from clients.

I may take a week or two break between contracts, but it's amazing how quickly people contact me when word gets around I am available. In my downtime I now make it very clear to people I'm having a breather. I may be doing some respite foster caring or working on developing my next opportunities in other aspects of my portfolio.

Success for me is very definitely when you take control to say when you want to work and when you want time off. *For example, after my father died I decided to take time off to travel with my mum. I have also had many extended weekends with my husband and you would never be able to do that in an employed job.*

Unlike the corporate world, where you tend to only meet and network with corporate people, another benefit and enjoyable aspect of having a portfolio career is the variety of people you meet. By working on projects in different industries and business sectors (e.g. public sector) it's a completely different group of people that you're mixing with. So, the breadth of the people you're surrounding yourself and engaging with is really different and energises you.

So, having a portfolio career might not suit everybody. However, **if you want to have a blend of what you want in your personal life as a result of the profit from doing things you really enjoy doing in your work life, then it is a great way to work and live!"**

Key Learning Points from Jane's story (Part 2)

- Passive income is beneficial in any portfolio career, especially regular income, e.g. from a property rental which can help fund other income streams, or become your main income

- Where clients really value your knowledge, experience and expertise you are in a great position to negotiate the work on your terms, e.g. when and how you work and your fees

- It is unlikely total perfection will be required – learn *'when good is good enough'*

- Building your support network and collaborations (with trusted like-minded people) can be greatly beneficial for any portfolio careerist

- The sum of the whole is greater than the parts and you can't do everything yourself

- Take great care when choosing people to collaborate with – it's your reputation on the line

- A portfolio career provides you an opportunity to develop a very different network – this will yield a great variety and diversity of connections as compared to corporate life

- It is unlikely you will need to cover all bases when you start your business

- Once you have planned thoroughly you can then bite the bullet and 'just do it'!

- For many people the portfolio lifestyle is about 'downsizing your career and upsizing your life' – you have choice as to what working lifestyle blend you create

Final Thoughts

Steve and Jane are both wonderful examples of how you can successfully redesign your career by embracing the portfolio career concept; equally important is the desire to achieve your working lifestyle blend. They have both truly adopted the portfolio lifestyle and despite no longer chasing work they are also both in constant demand. With Steve what is even more remarkable is he doesn't even have a website! All of his work is comes through recommendation and referrals.

With David, we have seen a completely different portfolio career approach, which certainly won't appeal to everybody but clearly works for him and showcases another aspect of what is possible.

The colourful umbrella approach is a great way to map out the different strands you would like to feature in your portfolio career and lifestyle. Just fill in the blanks as explained by Steve. Focus on the four key questions I have posed above to challenge your thinking and create your own colourful umbrella of choice. I really hope you also get similar inspiration as Steve did when completing this powerful exercise.

Jane has also proven you have the power to *'downsize your career and upsize your life'*, should you so desire. From whatever perspective you are looking at, the Portfolio career and lifestyle is an amazing and life-changing concept. What do you have to lose?

It's now time to move on to the final chapter. We have seen a common theme throughout the book of constant evolution and change. Read on for some remarkable and inspirational examples of why and how people have reinvented themselves, their careers and businesses.

CHAPTER 6

Reinvent – Change Means Reinvention

"The best way to predict the future is to create it."

Peter Drucker (1909-2005 – American management consultant, educator and author)

In this final chapter, you will meet a fascinating and diverse range of people who have all successfully reinvented themselves and their careers for different reasons. They have all very definitely created their futures. We will explore why each person chose to reinvent themselves and how they went about it. We will also explore some of the key elements that come into play when re-inventing yourself. Intentionally, many facets have already been covered in this book and this final chapter now allows me to draw these together and to highlight the importance of being able to 'Reinvent' yourself to have greater control over your destiny.

Creating a vision for your future

In order to reinvent yourself you need to be able to visualise what your future will look like and to share this with others in a compelling way. To challenge your thinking, here are some significant questions you will need to consider:

- What will I be doing in my business/portfolio career?

- How does this link to my values and needs?

- What research will I need to do?

- What learning/training will I need to make it happen?

- What new networks will I need to develop?

- How will I brand myself/what will I call myself or my business?

- What image do I want to portray?

- How will I position myself/what message do I want to get across?

- What marketing strategy do I need to adopt?

Rather than exploring these individually in detail, I will let the case studies do the talking and provide insightful suggestions to help drive you forward. It's possible that there is at least one other important question which may have crossed your mind as you have been reading through the book…

Is there an ideal type of person suited to reinventing themselves to develop a portfolio career?

I have highlighted repeatedly throughout the book that there is no 'one size fits all' approach. When you consider the amazing range and diversity of people featured in case studies, or mentioned briefly in examples, many are poles apart. They come from different backgrounds in terms of education, family upbringing, age groups, their previous careers and even from different parts of the globe. The case studies in this chapter alone will make this abundantly clear.

A client once said something that struck a chord; just before they went on to successfully develop their own unique work and life blend in their portfolio career:

"When one door closes, or you close it yourself, there are many other doors you can open"

...and this leads nicely into the next case study.

📖 *Case Study: Peter's Story*

Fusing Science, Business and Music

I had heard some fascinating stories from a number of contacts about Peter Cook and decided I just had to meet this character. I was able to join his LinkedIn group 'The Music of Business' as I was intrigued by the way he had combined two topics of great personal interest to me – 'Music' and 'Business'. Peter is a prolific writer and, like me, clearly enjoys challenging people to do better in the fields of leadership and management. He has had an unusual journey and portfolio career and became an obvious choice to interview for this book.

Peter is a 'polymath' who has fused several disciplines together. Not only is he a highly intelligent operator, but he is also such great fun. It's this unusual combination that allows him to influence and teach people whilst having a laugh at the same time. But even more impressively, I don't know of anybody who has had such an unusual career transition in their employed life and now an intriguing portfolio career that fuses his three passions. He has successfully combined Science, Business and Music to develop his company 'Human Dynamics and the Academy of Rock'.

It took a high degree of risk to pursue those passions and he has said:

"I think a lot of people who like the idea of self-employment don't adjust. I adjusted quite well but what I crucially did was to put myself in a critical situation by leaving a well-paid job at a difficult time for my family. I then had no choice but to prove to myself, the world and my wife that I would earn money out of this whole enterprise."

Peter has been a self-employed entrepreneur for over 23 years. During this time, he has become an author, written and contributed to 13 books on business leadership. Having won a prestigious prize for his work, awarded by Sir Richard Branson, he has since proudly accepted invitations to write, speak and deliver events for the Virgin.com brand.

Peter points out that his career has operated in 18-year cycles:

- 18 years in science, leading R&D teams to bring innovative pharmaceuticals to market and fixing factories on an international basis. This included the world's first treatments for HIV/AIDS, Herpes and the development of Human Insulin

- 18 years in academia, teaching MBAs to a diverse cadre of mature students and underpinning his industry experience

- 18 + years developing and running Human Dynamics and the Academy of Rock

- 18 x 3+ years playing music, which he fuses with science and business in his work

He takes up the story:

"Somewhat ironically I started out on April Fools' day 1994 running a conventional management consultancy called **Human Dynamics**. *We offered business consulting,*

training and coaching. To support the family, I also had an MBA tuition role at the Open University, which provided enough money to buy bread and butter."

Taking the leap of faith

"I more or less threw myself out of a well-paid job in pharmaceuticals, mortgaging the future at a difficult time – my wife was about to have our first baby. On reflection it was an incredibly sensible decision although some people criticised it at the time. The HR department at my company even suggested I was irresponsible and should stay on and 'keep taking the money'. They had not realised that we'd carefully considered the matter and, after long dialogue with my wife, we made the leap. She also left her job in the NHS at the same time, having disliked her boss and wanted to be a full time mother. We calculated that our money would last 18 months by living on 'Happy Shopper' beans etc. I would be the breadwinner and that if our experiment failed I would seek a full time job after a year. The first year was tough and I took £3,000 income, but the second rose by 600% and so on. 23 years later, two children and two recessions, I'm happy to quote Elton John... 'I'm still standing'."

Finding your USP (Unique Selling Proposition)

"At this early stage of my business, John Harvey Jones (the business guru), was quite popular on the television. He said that when he started out, doing what he did, he wore a dark suit and talked in a deep voice and tried to sound like someone from Price Waterhouse Coopers (PwC). I did much the same at the beginning. After a couple of years, I decided that I needed to be more of myself rather than following the herd. So I stumbled over the writing of my first book as a differentiator from the lunch budgets that the likes of PwC could offer. I also

started experimenting with a fusion of my passion for music with business development. My first book did indeed offer me a differentiator and so I started to follow this line of attack.

*Most people simply repeat their first book once they are successful, but I also chose differently. Having written a very worthy tome called 'Best Practice Creativity' as my first offering, I followed up with a riotously provocative book called 'Sex, Leadership and Rock'n'Roll', which blended my MBA with parallel lessons from my musical life. To my surprise I discovered that, not only did people want to read it, but they started to hire me to deliver keynotes and masterclasses that blended my passions for business and music. **I had found a hard to copy niche, perhaps by deliberation, but probably by accident.***

*So I set up a separate brand called the 'Academy of Rock' which specifically offered keynotes for busy people. I branded The Academy in a more exciting way than a traditional consultancy firm but avoided the air punching style of the keynote speaker tradition, opting for a differentiated blend of 'intelligent fun'. Since that time I've written and contributed to 13 books and have a vault of 3-5 more hidden away. **In the internet age it's important to have a brand as a self-employed business owner and continuously adapt and improve."***

Running the business

I asked Peter about how he manages the flow of business and where he places his effort. The reply was quite interesting. He said that Universities were quite eager to hire him as it turned out that he could run much more interesting lectures than their own people. Eventually he was doing so much work for little money that he adopted the strategy of 'cutting one arm off and seeing if another one grows', i.e. dropping high maintenance/low value business. He said:

"I really agonised about it the first time I did it because I felt that the arm will never re-grow, but it did eventually. I eventually killed off a lot of skills based training; I was good at it but it just wasn't a good use of my time. I raised my prices to discourage the public sector from using me. There is nothing worse than delivering employee development to people that have been 'sent there to learn', which is sometimes the case in such sectors. I'm only interested in people that really want to improve. This is both good for them and me as that almost guarantees they will get the outcomes they seek."

Business Planning

Peter has a very simple business planning process year-on-year.

"Annually I write down on one page what it is I want to achieve financially, operationally and emotionally. I give this to my wife who does a 'sanity check' on the plan. Once we have agreed we then let it happen. Simplicity is something that Sir Richard Branson also shares in his dealings with the Virgin group."

Balancing your portfolio

"My life currently divides about 50-50 between what I call 'short haul projects', i.e. keynotes for the Academy of Rock, and 'long haul projects' lasting 10-20 days over a year or longer, i.e. organisational consulting, where I'm there as a catalyst or provocateur. I call these two types of projects 'elephants' and 'fleas', following Charles Handy's analogy. In any given year I can handle a few elephants and a larger number of fleas."

Peter outlined some persistent challenges of running your own company:

"I almost exclusively work for larger companies such as Roche, Unilever, Fuji Film and The United Nations. One of the problems is that larger company's procurement departments are sometimes nervous to hire a small company. In my view they suffer from what I call the 'going to be run over by a bus' syndrome. In other words, a one-man band or micro business could be seen as a risk to large corporations or organisations that are used to working with large consultancies, with all their resources. It is also sometimes difficult to throw the resource behind what is needed to satisfy the bureaucracy. Therefore, I say 'no' to some requests if I think the costs of procurement outweigh the overall value of the work, e.g. Local Government.

If I had a magic wand I would invent a stick that could separate serious clients from the ones that simply want to get quotes in and benchmark themselves. I've spent countless hours providing free consultancy to people who have no intention of buying. Trouble is that you don't know that unless you enter the fray..."

Marketing

*"I've become quite good at managing my portfolio. I learned my marketing skills mainly through being the person that had to summarise the essence of the music bands I worked with. I condensed this onto a one inch square piece of paper for as a promotional leaflet and it was a great test. **If you cannot sum your business up on one small square of paper, you may miss opportunities with busy people.***

I've also become very good at using social media, although it's not as difficult as the 'so-called social media experts' claim. Over many years I've worked out the answer to the question: '50% of social media is a waste of time; the question is which 50%?' It seems that few people know the answer to this question, proof that hope is not a strategy for success.

I tell people that social media can be reduced to a question of 'numbers of people interested in what you do times the quality of what you have to say'. Both are important, but if you have quality content then numbers help you find the needle in the haystack, because it is a needle in a haystack if you run a niche business. So you have to have reasonable numbers to turn interest into work. I've become good at that as nearly half of my work now comes from people who I've never met face-to-face initially. Social media is only of value to a small business person if it contributes to business development. Otherwise it is just sharing cat pictures.

Not everything I've done has worked and most entrepreneurs recognise that trying stuff and failing is part of many people's journey to success. My most glorious failure was in sponsoring a world tour on the scale of the spoof rockumentary 'This is Spinal Tap' for a cult punk rocker, losing £40k into the bargain. This was in order to promote my 2nd book had the tour gone ahead. It failed not because it wasn't a good idea, but because of extremely poor execution by him and his tour team. They were economical with the truth on the state of the project and my big mistake was to give money to a friend. So the plane never took off, literally or metaphorically. This was a lesson in real life!"

Collaborations

"In reinventing myself, I've developed a lot of collaborations. These have included Sir Richard Branson's first business brain at Virgin Atlantic, David Tait OBE, Professor Adrian Furnham, author of around 90 books on psychology and Nadine Hack, who was instrumental in supporting Barack Obama and Nelson Mandela. The Academy of Rock side of my work has also morphed into working with class A rock stars, interviewing the likes of Roberta Flack, Prince's close musical family, Ozzy Osbourne's guitarist, John Mayall, the Godfather of the British Blues, AC DC, Bohemian Rhapsody's engineer et al. Some people think I lead a very interesting life as a result. I even got called up by CNN on the day that David Bowie died for an interview, possibly because Iggy Pop was not up at 7.30 am to take the call!

Collaborations matter, because, however much you would like to, there are some things you either cannot do or there is insufficient time to develop the competence. Bill Gates was allegedly not such a great manager but he was skilled at finding people who could do this for him. So don't spend loads of time trying to develop your weaknesses when you can acquire a range of people to make up for your weak spots."

Paying your dues

"I still love science and I find management sometimes is very poorly practiced. One would not be allowed to practice as a surgeon without an intimate knowledge of your field. Yet you are allowed to be a manager without such levels of deliberate practice. To be a great scientist or musician, you need your 10,000 hours of embedded learning. Great management is something that should be regarded as an art, which you practice to become good at. The same applies to everything I've tried to do in my life when I've wanted to be good at something.

It comes as a surprise to some people who don't know what I do. I think some of them believe I was a milkman one week, a barman the next week and a dustman the next before the rock and roll. It comes as a surprise that I spent 18 years in science, 18 years in academia and 18 years or plus running a business, that they're quite long, deep cycles of experience. I built up three pillars over a long time before stepping off to start this business. It's really quite important that you don't build your business on sand."

All work and no play

I asked Peter what he does to relax. Quite unsurprisingly music formed a part of his answer:

"I have made my hobby something that pays the bills so it's no surprise that I like to go out and jam to hone my musical skills. I prefer to go to a jam session and play with people I don't know to put something together and be a bit edgy. If there's a chance of things going wrong everyone learns a lot more about how to work with people, they pay attention better and so on. I also record music in my basement for my own consumption and anyone else who wants to listen to it. I need to have both. One for collaborative creativity and the other for solo creativity."

Why would I recommend this working lifestyle?

"Because you can enjoy what you do and if you don't – it isn't for everyone. But I'm quite driven by work and I like what I do. So therefore, I will stay up late and write a book if I haven't got time in the day to do it. I know so many people that don't succeed in the game of self-employment. If no one is managing them by having a deadline or they want something quickly, they don't do anything. For me, it's – you've got to be in this to do it your whole life. I've probably worked more hours than

I ever did when employed but I want to do it, so that doesn't feel like work to me.

Enjoy what you do, and don't do self-employment if you want to bump along as that's what will happen. If the numbers don't add up, it's painful. If you don't actually like the clients you're going to meet, it's painful. My decision to leave a well-paid job to start this business was as much informed by the famous 'Choose Life' T-shirt by Wham and the phrase 'Enjoy what you do' from 'Wham Rap'".

Key Learning Points from Peter's story

- Find your passion... then check to make sure people actually want to part with money for it!

- Establish your niche and find ways to clearly differentiate yourself from the competition

- It's important to have a brand as a self-employed business owner/portfolio careerist and continuously adapt and reinvent yourself as you follow your passions and values

- You can add or change strands to your portfolio as your business evolves

- Getting the right blend in your portfolio is important – too much low value/high maintenance work will stifle your opportunity to develop higher earning products or services

- It pays to write down and regularly review simple annual goals for you and your business – a mixture of financial and personal goals to achieve your desired objectives for the year

- Being able to quickly and easily explain your business to busy people will help gain opportunities – you don't need to share everything about your different portfolio strands

- Do the hard work – work is not work when you are working on what you love

- Collaborations matter and acknowledge that you can't always do it all by yourself

- Networking is key to finding likeminded people to pool strengths and help you with areas you wish to outsource

- If it's not fun, don't do it... enjoy what you do!

The next case study, like Peter, is another fascinating example of how you can shape different facets of your character and what you enjoy the most to create your portfolio career of choice.

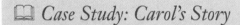 *Case Study: Carol's Story*

The 'Portfolio Director'

I met Carol Bode a few years ago at one of my Career Change & Transition Masterclasses. Having had a very distinguished career specialising in Organisational Development for Customer Service Industries of the private sector, she felt it was time for change. During the exercises to flesh out her interests, passions and talents, it became clear that along with her range of great skills and attributes Carol could create an interesting portfolio career. But like many people, Carol wasn't familiar with the portfolio career concept and hadn't realised that, inadvertently, she was already on the verge of starting one.

When I pointed this out to Carol she wasn't confident she could make it work for two reasons:

- Despite being a very talented photographer and having produced some wonderfully professional albums for various friends and family weddings, she saw photography as *'just a hobby and not something she could consider as an income stream'*

- Marketing was an issue. How could she market herself if she was doing a range of different things?

Both these points are typical concerns for many people considering a portfolio career and looking to reinvent themselves. Like so many aspects we have covered in the book, such concerns are essentially limiting beliefs and perception that can be overcome.

However, like many of the other examples in the book, Carol took a huge leap of faith by doing something completely different. She bit the bullet and set up her own Consultancy, moving into unchartered territory. The common denominator throughout her career has always been her love of working with people. She decided to utilise her leadership skills and other talents, along with her emerging passions for the health and housing sectors to create a portfolio career of her choice. Photography was still in the mix too. So the challenge now became the need to reinvent herself, marketing herself as widely as possible and to see what opportunities lay ahead.

Self-marketing / Positioning

My main reason for showcasing Carol was to demonstrate how she very cleverly positioned herself to create optimum impact. I invited Carol to be interviewed for this book following a profile change she has made on her LinkedIn profile. Carol had become *'The Portfolio Director'*. I loved this description but was equally intrigued by what this meant in reality in terms of her portfolio career. Carol takes up the story:

"You constantly play around with how you describe yourself. I started with thinking about what am I and what do I do? I went down the route of how do I describe I'm a board director who's held non-executive and executive roles and does other things as well? How do you capture all of the different things, especially on your LinkedIn profile?

Initially I came up with the 'Carol Bode Partnership'. The word partnership was really important to me because I don't want to just work on my own. A lot of my work is partnerships or collaborations with other people. I wanted this to be an umbrella for all of the stuff I do. However, the Carol Bode Partnership doesn't really mean anything to anybody.

Fast forward and I realised I do a portfolio of things. I like working at director level and I've got a portfolio of a number of director roles. So, I thought 'portfolio director'! That's how it evolved and then it just seemed to work.

I have learnt to expand on my brand and positioning to be clearer about my offering. So, on my LinkedIn profile I show my title as 'Portfolio Chair and Non-Executive Director'. On my LinkedIn Summary, I say I'm a 'Portfolio Director' and then describe this. The Carol Bode Partnership is really just the umbrella in terms of me and my business."

It is only since becoming a *'Portfolio Director* over the last 11 years that Carol has managed to reinvent herself. She has become a sought after Executive and Non-Executive Director in Health and Housing as well as a Chair of Governors for an Academy and Charity Trust. In addition, Carol also has her photography strand, mainly for portraits and weddings. She had previously created a separate website to market herself for her professional fee paying photographic work. However, as her portfolio has evolved, she has reverted back to only providing this service for family, friends and referrals on a mainly non fee 'giving' basis. Taking such an approach is therefore another example of how strands can change within your portfolio for different reasons, but for Carol her photography is still part of her 'colourful umbrella' and portfolio lifestyle.

Sensibly, Carol decided to only advertise her photographic services via her website and not as part of her LinkedIn profile. Keeping this separate from her Portfolio Director roles avoided any confusion and actually clarified her marketing position.

Decide for yourself what you feel about Carol's unique approach, but I personally love it. Knowing Carol and her range of skills, talents and passions, I feel *the Portfolio Director* approach is a perfect fit for her.

Key Learning Points from Carol's story

- Don't let the fear of how to market yourself hold you back from creating a portfolio career

- Carol is living proof that you can reinvent yourself within new business sectors with the right commitment, determination and marketing approach

- How you position yourself and your portfolio career can have a big impact on your success

- If you have a range of similar roles/strands within your portfolio, like Carol, then you have an opportunity to be creative with your branding and positioning

- As your portfolio evolves you may decide to switch the emphasis to certain key strands and downsize other activities

- It's fine to have passions you prefer to keep as mainly 'non-paid' but retain as part of your overall portfolio lifestyle – remember **you have choice**

- It is important you are comfortable being able to describe who you are and what you do

- As with so many things in life, **your success can often come down to what you say, how you say it and to whom**

That final emboldened statement provides a perfect link to our next case study as we meet someone whose portfolio career is based on that very sentiment.

📖 Case Study: Chris's Story

The LinkedIn Entrepreneur

I came across Chris J Reed as a result of exchanging comments regarding one of his numerous excellent blogs on LinkedIn. I was fascinated by his portfolio career and how he positions himself to stand out from the crowd. When reading about Chris it is important to realise that much of the work he now does, and the main strands of his portfolio career based around LinkedIn, would not have been possible or even existed before 2003.

Chris demonstrates that when you embrace the entrepreneurial spirit, it is possible to reinvent yourself, create a business from scratch, and turn it into something quite different, yet special. The fact Chris talks about *'passion portfolios'* says it all for me. His overview alone makes interesting reading and you might need to pause for breath, afterwards!

Chris is the Founder & Global CEO of Black Marketing; a global marketing consultancy that specialises in enabling LinkedIn for C-suite Executives & Entrepreneurs across the world. He has taken the company from 1 person in 1 country in 2014 to a full listing on the NASDAQ in 2016.

Chris has many other claims to fame, most notably as the only NASDAQ Listed CEO with a Mohawk hairstyle. He has also been named as an Official LinkedIn Power Profile 2012-2016, having one of the world's most viewed LinkedIn profiles with over 70,000 followers, No. 1 in Singapore, hundreds of recommendations, one of the top 100 most influential LinkedIn Bloggers, and a No. 1 International Best Selling Author with his book 'LinkedIn Mastery for Entrepreneurs'.

In his words *"My late Grandad always told me that success was not what you know, it was who you know"* and LinkedIn has proved him right. Chris is also an experienced event speaker and chairperson for conferences, company events and regularly holds LinkedIn workshops.

Chris writes passionately about all aspects of marketing and business for various media brands. He has been featured in various books and is heavily involved with the Singapore Management University Mentorship programme for final year marketing students at SMU's Business School. This is an unpaid voluntary part of his portfolio that, from my interview with him, is clear this is work he really values to help inspire and develop future entrepreneurs.

Phew… So, let's meet Chris and understand more about his motivation. Why a 'Geordie' lad from the northeast of England ended up in Singapore and why he does what he does today.

What made me decide to leave the UK and move away from my previous business career?

"A mixture of reasons really. One of them was the fact I was an entrepreneur in the UK who wanted to be an entrepreneur in Asia. I wanted to test myself over here and have more flexibility, but also more empowerment in terms of working for myself. However, there was also a catalyst… two previous employers who didn't pay me! I had to basically sue them to get the money I was rightly owed. I also didn't want to be in a position ever again where I'm relying on somebody else to pay me, especially in a country, in a different region such as Asia, for example, compared to the UK and Europe.

This meant I had more control over who paid me, who I worked for and what I did. **Taking back control also meant I could actually build a business of my own, as opposed to making money for other people, and flexibility to express my passions for other things.**

I now have the flexibility to work how I want. Today in Hong Kong, next week in Manila, the week after I'm in Shanghai and then back home to Singapore. So I have the flexibility to move around because it's my business. I also want to develop it how I want to and I couldn't do that if I worked for somebody else. You'd have to get approval for this and approval for that. But having a passion for the business and owning it yourself, there's nothing quite like it."

In the business of connecting

"When I first came to Singapore I knew no one. I therefore reached out on LinkedIn to ask people to introduce me to people they knew in Singapore. They did. I got my first, second and third jobs in Singapore through connecting with people on LinkedIn.

None of these jobs actually existed or were advertised before I connected and met the people in charge. They were created for me because, having met me, they thought I fitted the vision of where the business was going and my skills, personality and experience inspired them to create the job for me. It all happened through networking.

All these roles are regional roles which meant I started using LinkedIn even more to find the right people in Asia Pacific to connect with, message and talk to. China, India, Japan, Australia, Kuala Lumpur, Jakarta, you name it. I could find a Chief Marketing Officer (CMO) of a brand in that country using LinkedIn. By using LinkedIn, I was also able to find decision makers, Chief Executives, CMOs, people who had budgets and won them as clients. LinkedIn enabled me to build a pipeline that I could not have done any other way across Asia Pacific.

I quickly realised that aside of reaching out to people on LinkedIn to find key connections, you can also use LinkedIn to win business and find jobs as well.

So I started doing training and I started getting asked to do training across the world in LinkedIn. Then people started asking me to pay them for managing their LinkedIn accounts. I saw there was a business opportunity, here in Singapore, the same way as when I was an entrepreneur in the UK. I can live my passion for connecting myself and other people socially to help senior executives and entrepreneurs also connect when they don't have the time, experience, or the expertise to do it themselves. Hence, my Black Marketing company was formed."

How did I develop my portfolio career?

I started developing a portfolio career. It basically came out of people contacting me saying, "I want to work with you, I can see your talents, I can see your experience, I can see your contacts, but I can't afford your rates." So I thought there's got to be another way of doing this. I'll create a company which basically controls stakes in companies or has stakes in companies. We don't take cash payments, we take share payments, so we get paid in shares. Therefore, we have a stake in the company. If the company does well and it uses our Black Marketing LinkedIn services, then we do well because we could then sell our stake and we can make more money than by just getting fees. If we don't do very well for them, they have the option to buy back our stake at competitive or nominal rates.

Essentially, I'm taking a gamble based on my experience and my faith in my Black Marketing company's ability to drive business for other people, because you're not getting paid. So therefore it is really a passion. It's not something you sweat equity for. You could call it a 'passion equity', if such a term exists. Thereby, I'm saying I believe in you as a person and a business. You just need some help in terms of your LinkedIn. Therefore, I'll help you, but in return you're giving me a stake of the business. We have a wide range of businesses where we have stakes that I wouldn't otherwise be involved in. They range from content marketing, social media marketing, digital marketing, to wine, yoga, management consulting and leadership training. I'm very open to the idea because of the fact I have a real passion to help other entrepreneurs.

Another real passion of mine is speaking. These requests are also coming from mainly in Asia. People didn't really know how to use LinkedIn, so they turn to me and say 'How do you use LinkedIn? Can you do a talk about it?' And that turned into 'Can you do a workshop?' And that turned into 'Can you come to, Kuala Lumpur, Jakarta, Bangkok, Sydney, Shanghai, Guangzhou or Hong Kong to present?'.

<u>This is fantastic. I get to talk about my passion, I get to travel the world, meet some great people, and they'll pay me at the same time! And it helps my LinkedIn business too. What more could I ask?"</u>

What is my main business income stream?

"This is definitely Black Marketing. I started Black Marketing a couple of years ago in Singapore with one person, and now it's 35 people in 9 different countries. So that's the real premium breadwinner; dealing with C-Suite executives and getting paid to develop their

LinkedIn profiles, their personal profiles, their company profiles, their personal brand, their company brand, their content marketing strategy, and win them new business. That is really the key to success in all the other ventures because it helps fund all the other ventures. So if Black Marketing wasn't doing very well, I couldn't afford to have the other passion portfolios."

What do I do in the way of voluntary work in my passion portfolio?

"The voluntary stuff is with the Chambers. So I do a lot for both the American Chamber of Commerce in Singapore and the British Chamber of Commerce in Singapore and am on a number of committees. What I love about this work is we're putting on events for the members and seeking out speakers who are experts in their field. We don't get paid for it, we do it for the profile, we do it for the engagement. We also do it as we have passion to hear what other people have to say, and a passion for really listening and learning to experts in various fields.

On the British Chamber, I'm in the ICT committee, the entrepreneur committee, and the marketing committee. Therefore, this covers my three passion areas, which is amazing! I help the chamber build, help the British and the American companies build in Singapore and basically help the members learn a lot more things. This also involves another passion, networking, which is fantastic because you meet so many interesting people. Essentially, getting involved in these Chambers is kind of like a labour of love.

I'm also a mentor for SMU, which is Singapore Management University final year graduates, and I open that up for other people, other marketing graduates as well. I do various speeches too at different universities.

I often get people coming up to me afterwards asking if I will mentor them. Of course it's a pleasure to do so. As long as they're not working for Microsoft, Google or something like that, it's really good because you're giving something back as well. You also get to see them grow and they'll always remember you helped them grow. So, when they become Chairman or Chief Executive of Google, I hope they will still remember me and what I have done for them!"

Expat life in Singapore

"It's very easy being an expat in Singapore. It's much easier in Singapore than places such as Hong Kong or Shanghai, because it's English-speaking first. In Hong Kong it is very difficult to even communicate with taxi drivers. Singapore is very much a western society with around a third of the population not Singaporean but expats of one kind or the other. It's also a multi-cultural, multi-racial society, which gives equal weight to all religion or races and it deliberately has policies to make sure there's no friction.

You're always going to get some people complaining about expats being over here to steal local jobs, but that's rarely the case. All the jobs I've created as a business owner didn't exist before and I'm giving equal weight to expats, just as important to Singaporeans. There's lots and lots of rules and regulations in terms of who can apply for jobs and how many Singaporeans you have to employ. However, with unemployment around 1%, actually, there's full employment here, so people can pick and choose. So it's a great place to work, and also because it's very much a hub of Asia. It's very much the place where people use as a regional base, so it's wonderful to be an expat here."

Would I ever go back to a typical one company employed role?

"No, never in a million years, never! **I'd rather work myself and fail, than work for somebody else and succeed. Because even succeeding with somebody else does not give you the same satisfaction of trying to work for yourself.** *Even if things don't work for yourself, you learn so many lessons. You just make sure you don't make those mistakes the next time and then you can build a business as a result.*

I've been an entrepreneur for over 20 years, on and off, and it's fantastic, especially in Asia. Therefore, I am never ever going back to work for somebody else. Working for yourself enables you to be more positive and actually work for who you want to, when you want to and have more control. You can travel when you want to and you can do what you want – just as long as you have the business fundamentals and foundation in place. It's important to have good people around you."

Why Passion, Pleasure and Profit in that order?

"I firmly believe that you have to be passionate about what you do. The most miserable people you ever meet are people who make a lot of money but aren't very passionate about what they do. So, you have to be passionate about what you do. I'm very lucky in that I've worked in the music industry, TV and radio as well. I'm very passionate about music and I've worked in sports and for internet and various different industry newspapers, magazines, where I was absolutely passionate about what the work I did.

Having a passion for something is brilliant. However, combined with it being your passion and building it because you're passionate about the business, is

even better. *I get a lot of pleasure for doing LinkedIn myself. I get pleasure from doing it for other people. I get pleasure in combining both LinkedIn with building up somebody else's business and getting paid for it which enables me to make a profit.*

If I turned that around and I said 'how am I going to make a profit first?' I might as well just go into banking or financial services because you're not getting a lot of enjoyment. You've got a lot of stress, and that's not what I ever want. **I always want to be passionate and never think about work as being work, that's the key to being an entrepreneur.**

I think you always look at your pleasure and your passion and your work as the same thing. It's not a chore to do the work. You don't mind doing it on Saturdays, you don't mind doing it on Sundays. You don't mind getting involved and getting stuck in and rolling up your sleeves and working late if you have to, and networking, because you're building a business. And that's really because it's pleasurable.

I love meeting new people and developing businesses for them. I can't imagine just going out there and thinking okay, I need to make money, I need to make money, because that is not very pleasurable. It's also very stressful because you're putting an undue burden on yourself. Whereas, if you work for your passions, the profit will come. <u>*Because you're so committed and you're so passionate about what you do, the profit comes along automatically, providing your business model is right, your service model is right and as long as your fundamentals' are right."*</u>

What does success mean for me?

"In summary, I would say it goes back to what my granddad said, 'it's not what you know, it's who you

know'. Having a 'passion portfolio', you work with people you want to, you help people you really want to. **You get a lot of pleasure from working with people you like, doing work you like and getting a lot of advocates. That's really the key.** *Life's very short and if you can also help other people build their businesses at the same time, then that's fantastic. It's win-win!"*

Key Learning Points from Chris's Story

- With the right mindset, belief and positive action, it is possible to reinvent yourself and create a new business and 'passion portfolio' in a completely different country and culture

- Singapore is a country that embraces entrepreneurial spirit but do your 'homework' first

- The power of LinkedIn cannot be underestimated – it's your main shop window to the world to develop and optimise your networks, also to open up and create new work opportunities

- By becoming an expert, you can create income streams sharing your knowledge to help benefit other people and there are always spin-off benefits to other aspects of your portfolio

- Inspirational and motivational specialist speakers are always in demand – even better if you can travel the world and get paid for sharing your passion

- Any voluntary aspect of your portfolio can also add kudos to your brand and reputation

- If your passions feature as strands of business and you are also passionate about developing your business, you have the ideal winning combination

- Success is not what you know... it's who you know!

For an inspirational finale to the main chapters of the book, let's now revisit Gail Gibson, from Chapter 4, to learn how she is planning for the next remarkable phase in her portfolio career and lifestyle.

📖 *Case Study: Gail's Story Part 2*

Embracing Variety, Choice and Change to live the dream!

"As I approach the achievement of 11 years in business, I take a moment to reflect on three key aspects – variety, choice and change.

Since I began my entrepreneurial journey in 2005, my business has grown, changed, grown further and changed several times. Why? Because variety is the spice of why I do what I do. Variety is about the people I choose to work with. Variety is about the different style of work I deliver to my clients. Variety helps my focus, my productivity, my creativity and the fun I get from doing what I do as a performance coach.

Choice is the reason why I now offer my services as a performance coach. Now in my 9th year as a coach, the choices I've made along the way have led to evolving my unique style and approach. I now deliver outdoor performance coaching programmes for professional women and female entrepreneurs.

Faced with an opportunity to reinvent myself and my business, I chose to combine my passion for running and my love of the outdoors with my style of performance coaching, to help individuals perform better in life, career and business.

Change I embrace with wide open arms. I thrive on change. I need change because it keeps me on my toes.

It challenges how I develop my programmes. Change continues to help me help others to make their dreams happen. It's all about flexibility, being adaptable, facing your fear (and doing it anyway) and believing in yourself."

Variety, choice and change

"These are three of my best friends who will join me on the next stage of my life and business journey, to Malaysia. My friends and I will make connections, develop ideas, build programmes, deliver training and coaching and move my life closer to truly living my dream.

I plan to set up a lifestyle design opportunity out there, getting to know a network with the local community when I first go out there. I would like to offer my services maybe with a local charity, perhaps copywriting, social media, or business development opportunities for them on a voluntary basis."

Developing and opening up new networks

"As my portfolio continues to morph and change, the move to Malaysia is stepping up a gear. In preparation, I am now making use of my network to develop and build relationships with people in South East Asia. I am doing this because introductions are powerful and can lead to exciting new opportunities and ways of thinking, on which I thrive. Making new connections now helps to shift my focus and commitment to another level. These connections will open doors to new beginnings, both for myself and my husband.

One fantastic networking opportunity, Rare Birds, has exploded my plans into action. I've been following the growth of the Rare Birds brand since their inception in 2014. The Rare Birds 'moon-shot' (vision) is to empower 1,000,000 women globally to become entrepreneurs by 2020. Excited by the prospect and being opportunistic in approach, I made contact with them in 2015 and signed up as a Mentor. Mid 2016 I had a successful Skype interview with a Rare Bird ambassador, which then led to my profile being matched with a female entrepreneur in Perth, Western Australia, my hometown. From November 2016, for a period twelve months, I have now embarked on a journey of personal and business discovery with my Rare Bird mentee, via weekly Skype mentor sessions. I'm loving the experience.

Linking to Rare Birds is an ideal way to extend my network into the Australasian region. In addition, there is a potential role as a Rare Birds Ambassador once I'm established."

A new life for us both

"Having also had an extensive portfolio career throughout his working life, my husband Shaun, is now approaching the end of almost 20 years as a reservist in the RAF. His portfolio includes chef, security, photographer, first aid instructor and martial arts enthusiast. As he considers the next stage, and as we explore our Malaysian opportunities, Shaun is enthusiastic about his choices ahead. With a wide variety of transferable skills in his toolkit, his next move can be one of **choice**. Already his passion to cook is resurfacing, as he is keen to open a bar/grill with a Western focus, or teach Western style cooking. He'd also like to explore leadership training with a military twist."

Shared vision for our next life chapter

"Our shared vision for Malaysia is to create a lifestyle hub where people can co-work (Digi nomads), learn (personal and business development), or simply be (eat, drink, relax). Together, we believe we can make our dream happen, for ourselves, and for people who buy into and who want to be part of our dream too."

Key Learning Points from Gail's story (Part 2)

- Variety, choice and change can become your 'best friends' and shape your future portfolio career and lifestyle

- To reinvent yourself or your business you must first create your vision, then fill in the gaps and take positive action to make it happen as Gail is now doing with her move to Malaysia

- Regardless of where you are planning to work in the world, making new connections and developing new networks will be key to your success

- Associating yourself with great causes that are in tune with your values, and where you can add value with your skill set, can open up a whole new world of possibilities for you

- If you are planning on a major lifestyle change and move to another country, having a shared vision with your partner will help to create excitement and the momentum to make your dream become reality

Final Thoughts

What a wonderful way to finish this final chapter before we move into the conclusion with a potentially amazing lifestyle transformation in the making. To turn your dream into reality, like everything in life, takes bags of determination, commitment, belief and positive action. Knowing Gail, as I do, I have absolutely no doubt she will make it happen. I'm sure Gail and her husband will soon be continuing the next chapter of their portfolio career and lifestyle journey in Malaysia.

Reinvention is rarely easy, but it can be exciting and reinvigorating and can provide the impetus for a new lease of life. Sir Richard Branson is often hailed as 'the master of reinvention'. He is well known for his thoughts that people, and especially businesses, should never stand still but constantly embrace change and reinvent themselves. This is no different with portfolio careerists. Peter, Carol, Chris and Gail are all excellent examples that demonstrate why people have chosen to reinvent themselves and ultimately their businesses. Naturally they all had different reasons and adopted slightly different approaches – but they have all been successful.

As we move towards the conclusion, I'm sure you have now gathered a huge bag of different types of 'sweets' ready to taste. Just as I suggested back in Chapter 1, you've now picked and mixed so many ideas from the selection provided throughout this book that you could be spoilt for **choice**. But nonetheless, a **choice** you are far better equipped to now make. Let Passion, Pleasure and Profit be your drivers for success.

So be ready to feast your eyes on the final revelations to follow... before you go out into the world to unwrap those opportunities and savour your own unique portfolio career and lifestyle.

CONCLUSION

"There is no greater thing you can do with your life and your work than follow your passions in a way that serves the world and you."

Sir Richard Branson
(British Entrepreneur, business magnate, investor,
philanthropist and founder of the Virgin Group)

What a fabulous quote to sum up my sentiments in writing this book and the concept of changing your working lifestyle by working for the 3 Ps of **Passion, Pleasure** and **Profit!**

As you have journeyed through the different chapters, meeting many remarkable people, learning from their stories, reading my memoirs and absorbing the general wealth of information, can you imagine what it will be like to now follow a similar path as some of the people you have met along the way?

We have seen many fascinating success stories and different types of portfolio careers, but we have also seen struggles where things haven't quite gone to plan. Think about your favourite case studies and why they resonated with you?

What do you now need to make your portfolio career become a reality?

A portfolio career isn't for everybody. However, if you hadn't realised it before reading this book, the portfolio career really is a wonderful alternative working lifestyle where you can enjoy Mondays as much as Fridays. With this book, I have given you the ammunition and provided inspiration to make it happen. _It's now up to you as it is within your reach._

We've had a good look at the changes that are facing us in the world of work. We have explored the 3 Ps and also the 3 Cs. I'm sure you will have already drawn your own conclusions from the book, but maybe you are still wondering… _what are the things that really make the difference when looking to create a successful Portfolio Career?_

<u>Rev</u>elations – The difference that makes the difference!

What do the successful case studies in the book have in common?

There are numerous aspects that set the successful people apart. This is probably a book in itself! However, I am going to offer the top 10 factors, from a mixture of my extensive experience and the learning from the case studies. I believe these create the biggest impact in making a successful transition into a portfolio career and then for your continued success. You could argue that all 10 are equally important. So, although they are in a relative priority order, focus on them all.

Interestingly, a number of these factors appear to be inherently intuitive, as shown in many of the case studies. Therefore, the top 5 are covered in greater detail, as the rest are more self-evident. _It is worth noting that the first factor is the only one totally specific to portfolio careers. The rest are all significant_ *factors towards achieving success in any aspect of business, career or life transition.*

1. Find Your Anchor

Having worked with many people over the years and developed the reputation of being 'The Career Catalyst', I have gained a real sense of what works, when creating a portfolio career. This first key factor is something that acts as ballast and in effect becomes the mainstay to help secure the foundations of your portfolio career. *What is it?...*

"Find one key strand that initially allows you to secure and guarantee regular work. This should help cover most of your bills and allow you to focus and develop other income strands alongside"

I'm sure you will agree this simple but effective approach makes perfect sense. You will find the majority of people featured in the case studies have either consciously or unconsciously adopted this principle. I call this 'finding your **anchor**'. *Why?* Because of a particularly striking response given by a client who had a sudden eureka moment when I shared the portfolio career concept with her. I remember her excitedly saying… "*I get it. I will find **'my anchor'** and I can then spread my wings and develop other passions and strands of work I love alongside this*".

The very use of this powerful metaphor both inspired and drove her forward in making a career transition; the sturdy grounding for the launch of her successful portfolio career of choice working for the 3 Ps.

Marc, the comedy writer we met briefly in Chapters 3 and 6, sums up this approach:

"My anchor always used to be the business admin side of things, which paid for me to develop the comedy writing and other creative sides of my portfolio. But now it's more evenly balanced because in the last couple of years, as a writing team,

we have managed to get much more regular work. So that's helped, because it places less pressure on me in general, but also less pressure on making one thing a success. However, the anchor was invaluable to begin with. It definitely helps because if you want to let your imagination run free, it is difficult to think about creating something if you're under real financial pressure. So having an anchor helps remove that level of anxiety."

As with Marc, you could end up with more of an even spread across your strands as your portfolio career evolves. Furthermore, you have the choice and flexibility to allow your anchor to change and exploit new opportunities that may come along. I have constantly done this myself. Regardless, as an important starting point I have often said, **"Go find your anchor then spread your wings!"**

2. Mindset

"Whether you think you can or you can't, you're right."

Henry Ford
(1863-1947 – American industrialist
and founder of the Ford Motor Company)

'Mindset' has been mentioned repeatedly throughout this book as well as in my previous books, audio books and online programmes. I have proven time and again, having 'the right mindset' is a significant factor in achieving a successful portfolio career, or indeed any sustainable transition.

In Chapter 2 we looked closely at the impact of 'conditioning' or restricted thinking brought about as a result of a number of factors and influences in your life. Change your thinking, change your life. So carefully reconsider Henry Ford's quote and realise that mindset is the very essence of what will determine whether you succeed or fail. *Focus on what you want – not what you don't want or fear!*

We have established there is no one ideal type of person, age or talent required to create a successful portfolio career.

What is most important is that you have the right mindset. Shifting a fixed mindset is key in allowing you to move from the conditioned thinking of an 'employed job' to one of 'open possibility'. The wonderful examples in this book are testament to this, especially how people have changed their mindset to change their results and their life. It isn't always easy to achieve this shift on your own. Like many of the examples, you may feel there is benefit in working with a specialist career coach to help make that change happen for you.

Resilience is also a common thread running throughout the book; another key aspect of mindset. As we have seen, creating your portfolio career is unlikely to be plain sailing and there will inevitably be highs and lows. Managing the emotional roller coaster ride takes resilience. Both Julian and Gail make particular mention of this in Chapter 4. Therefore, enjoy and celebrate the highs whilst staying positive, proactive and opportunistic during the lows.

The completion of this book has been a 2 year emotional roller coaster ride for me in view of various intervening factors, not least the passing of my best friend Don (Chapter 1). He was so excited to be involved at the outset, but tragically never had a chance to do anything other than thank me for the opportunity. However, I have been resilient and determined to bounce back and make this book a reality, just as Don would have wanted.

In writing and compiling the book I have found reading through the case studies to be highly inspirational, as I trust you have too. It has been hugely rewarding to learn of the many new evolutions, career and lifestyle successes that have happened since my original interviews with the people featured. Everyone involved with the book has remained keen to see how it has evolved and are eager to read the final product. The case studies consistently demonstrate great resilience in overcoming obstacles and embracing their challenges. Not an easy thing to do, but their reward is now enjoying a rich, blended working lifestyle of their choice in working for *Passion, Pleasure and Profit*. Hand on heart they can honestly say *they love Mondays as much as Fridays*, as you can too. I applaud them all.

People often ask me whether having a *portfolio career* means you need to have greater self-belief and greater resilience than people who have an *employed job?* This is an interesting question and my view is clear. I believe you need self-belief in any role to make it a success. However, when looking to pursue a portfolio career you will need an inner-strength, determination and confidence to think differently to achieve your goals. I have heard statements of self-doubt such as *"People won't take me seriously because I do a range of different things"*. This is a limiting belief and mindset shift people have to make. What is most important is doing what you want and taking control of your career. If you love what you do, are good at what you do and people want to buy different strands of your products or services, then this is what really matters. So, such thinking and beliefs need to be part and parcel of a positive and resilient mindset to thrive working for the 3 Ps.

3. Managing Your Portfolio

Another great question I get asked regularly is, *"What happens when different strands of your portfolio become overloaded, or you have deadlines that start to overlap?"*

Before I respond, let's pause momentarily to allow you to consider how you might tackle such perceived 'dilemmas'. If you're like me, you could be thinking, "Hey, what a great problem to have, I must be doing something right". So, yet again, we are back to mindset but this time with a twist.

There are always solutions to any challenge. As with most as aspects of working life, **how you plan, organise and prioritise things** (in this case workload and resources) will make a real difference.

The answers to the question also lie in some of the examples provided in many of the cases studies:

- **Negotiate** or clarify the completion date of projects – Don't assume 'urgent' really means urgent, as experience has proven how few times this is the case

- **Be honest with yourself** – Delegate or outsource tasks or projects you prefer not to do or that could be done better and more timely by others as time = money for you and your clients/customers

- **Collaborate** with known and trusted people to utilise their talent and provide a cohesive team effort. Collaborations are a great way forward for many portfolio careerists. *The sum of the whole is greater than the parts.* It can also be great fun working with like-minded people, pooling talents and resources. This often leads to creative ideas and opportunities.

The late Steve Jobs summed it up for me saying, ***"Believing the dots will connect down the road will give you the confidence to follow your heart".***

4. Taking Positive Action

"Success goes where your energy flows "

The 6th and final step of my Career Navigation Cycle process and again an essential ingredient for success in life. Steve, in Chapters 3 and 5, shares his learning and constant surprise that by **taking positive action will 'create ripples in the universe'.** I have also known Steve to say, "You cannot change the law of physics", and he often refers to Newton's 3rd Law:

"For every action, there is an equal and opposite reaction".

No Action = Nothing Happens
(maintain the steady state – no change)

Action = Reaction (energy generating the 'Ripple Effect')

Creating a portfolio career can be scary and or exciting. Either way, follow up and follow through with positive action to create those ripples in the universe, as the examples in this book have done. I will re-iterate the point… **only you can take responsibility for your career and life.** Therefore, as well as being passionate about the work you do, **what will really make the difference is also learning to love putting in the work to make it happen.** This then becomes a winning combination. As with the Nike adage, 'Just Do It'!

5. Self-marketing, Networking and Social Media

"You don't want to be an island… You need to 'be out there'"

LinkedIn is the professional version of Facebook and a must for all professionals and executives to maximise your online presence and brand, also develop and optimise your networks. Likewise, Twitter and Facebook are also enormously helpful to generate new followers and advocates for your work. However, it's important to carefully combine online with face-to-face networking to ensure you have the opportunity to build connections and rapport in person. Admittedly the latter is more time consuming and has limited reach, but a balance of the two will improve your chances of success and the human element can often make the difference.

Chris J Reed, the LinkedIn expert and entrepreneur featured in Chapter 6, is a firm believer in the benefits and principles of networking and social media. In making your portfolio career a success, he says: *"It's all about who you know. Who you're connected with, who's your second connection, who's your third connection, who could introduce you, how you are known and how good your reputation is. As long as you have good contacts and a good reputation you will go far. Also, you should always make sure you don't burn bridges and act professionally at all times".* I could not agree more with this very sound advice.

Like some of the other case studies, I have also found by becoming a recognised thought leader in your field or showcasing your talents (as with Tara and her art in Chapter 2) combined with tactical use of social media, can give you a global presence. I marvel when interviews for radio shows, podcasts, newspapers, blogs and business journals, can then go viral when shared on social media. Such activity and publicity can suddenly catapult your reach enabling you to develop a global audience for your products and services.

We saw in Chapter 2 how technology is having a massive impact on how we work. Couple this with social media and it becomes possible to open up new channels of business and income streams, which would have been inconceivable a decade or so ago. However, **this will only happen by taking positive action.**

6. Clarity, Focus and Goals

"You can't hit a target you can't see"

Although some people just go with the flow, the case studies have proven being clear on why you want to create a portfolio career and what outcomes you desire, means you can then set specific goals to achieve them. Having such clarity and focus also makes it much easier for you to also explain to other people what you do and why you do it, another key ingredient for success.

7. Establish Your True Worth and Confidently Charge it

All too often I have seen people making the mistake of being too charitable, plain naive or just not having the confidence to charge their true worth. It is important for your professional integrity and reputation to charge what you are worth, regardless of how important the financial aspects of your portfolio are. You can always find other ways to be charitable and give back, such as voluntary work.

8. Planning, Research and Due Diligence

As with everything in life, planning is key to success and research is a key part of any planning to create your portfolio career. Regardless of what you decide to do and the risk involved there will inevitably be a need for considerable research. Where significant investment is involved then significant due diligence is also essential.

9. Ongoing Learning and Development

Many people cite continual learning as one of the main benefits of having a portfolio career. Being involved in different activities with a diverse range of clients or customers inevitably promotes learning. In addition, having a focus on developing personally and professionally will pay dividends. The biggest learning often comes from your mistakes. We are all human, so remember it is okay to make mistakes **but don't make the same mistake twice!**

10. Think Like an Entrepreneur

I know many people who have portfolio careers who don't consider themselves to be remotely entrepreneurial. However, being opportunistic, open to change, re-invention and exploring synergies with like-minded people are definitely all key traits for successful portfolio careerists. Therefore, you too can think like an entrepreneur.

"Advantage... Portfolio Careerist!"

Here's a brief story that encapsulates many of the key points featured in this book and poignantly highlights my purpose in writing it.

Game

True to the values and principles of my portfolio lifestyle, I took a break from writing the book conclusion to play a local league tennis match with Paul. We hadn't met before. Afterwards he said how much he enjoyed the game and also how pleased he was to have taken additional time off work following the Christmas/New Year period, because he had become 'so *stressed out'*. I was intrigued by this comment, so asked him what he did for a living. Paul then shared some remarkable insights. If you believe things happen for a reason, then our chat was clearly meant to be – his points were quite thought provoking in bringing this conclusion together.

It transpired Paul was a manager in a global financial services company in the City of London. He admitted to having a highly stressful job and yet had only taken one week's leave from the previous year's entitlement. As his story unfolded it became clear that work pressures were taking a toll on his health and well-being; problems reminiscent of the research undertaken by the CMI in Chapter 2. Why would you put persistent job demands above your own health?

This was my cue to explain the nature of my work. I shared an example of one of my most memorable career change success stories. It was all the more poignant because my client did exactly the same job as Paul. I explained how my client became so stressed and distraught that one lunchtime she just got up and walked out, never to return! For some time she had dreamt about following her true passion to become a paramedic and finally decided to 'just do it'. She overcame many obstacles but her determination, commitment and positive mindset made it happen. But would Paul be **game** enough to reconsider his options and to have the courage to try something new?

Set

Paul was intrigued and became quite thoughtful. Although to date his mind has been **set** on a fixed employed job in financial services, he admitted to having thought about giving this up to become a gardener. I found myself telling him about my best friend Don and how his case study featured in Chapter 1 of this book. I explained how gardening was just one part of Don's extensive portfolio career and doing work he truly loved. Paul was eager to know more as I could tell he was itching to break free from his corporate shackles. However, it was also evident he was clearly suffering from the deep rooted conditioning and fears often experienced when confronting career change.

Match

He was unfamiliar with the portfolio career concept, so I began to suggest a way forward for him, this book being the start point. He was even more intrigued and asked me about the book. I explained the significance of the title. By now he looked totally stunned and enquired, *"What do you mean by working for passion pleasure and profit?"*. I naturally shared what you now know.

As we left he thanked me and said, *"This has been inspirational. Such a valuable and different conversation from those I normally have with people"*. We agreed to keep in contact, so it will be interesting to see how his story unfolds in the future. Having been taken aback by his parting comments, I really do hope he becomes one of the first people to read this book and become inspired to choose to redesign his career and reinvent himself as a portfolio careerist. I think he would be a perfect **match**.

People like Paul are the reason I wrote this book – I wanted to share my knowledge and learning to make a difference to people's lives for the better. I have repeatedly said that one of the most significant aspects of having a portfolio career is that you have **choice**. With the flexibility and freedom this working lifestyle affords, you can determine:

- The type of work you do

- When you work

- Where you work

- Who you work with

- How you work with others

We all have great **Passion** within us – it's a question of liberating this emotion and harnessing it to achieve what you truly want in life. We gain much **Pleasure** from the things we enjoy in life – what we love doing is so satisfying and provides bliss. But by combining these two powerful components in a work sense, you can then derive the financial rewards and **Profit. The '3 Ps' really is a life changing concept.**

"And finally…"

Can you remember the cover of this book, with the birds? Was there was something that caught your eye and resonated with or maybe you never really studied the cover? It's no doubt been a while since you turned that first page. The following explains the metaphor:

The fledglings have now long since flown and left the nest. They found new freedom and their way in life through curiosity and having the courage to try new things. They may have stumbled initially, but have since grown in stamina and stature having fed on the knowledge they gathered along the way. They have learnt how to survive and thrive, even in the most inhospitable environments, once their ambitions had been realised. With wings fully unfurled, and a growing sense of confidence, they are now soaring to achieve new heights and show others the way. Spiralling ever upwards and not looking back.

I'm wondering if you realise just how much you have learnt from this book and how well equipped you now are to achieve your own personal transformation into a portfolio career of your choice? There's no more to think about… fly high, soar… 'Just Do It!'

I would value your review

Now you have completed the book, in order to spread the word about portfolio careers and working for Passion, Pleasure & Profit, I would be most grateful for and value your honest review on Amazon.

STEVE'S

Inspirational Career & Personal Development Resources

Portfolio Careers & Lifestyle

Breakthrough Career Coaching with Steve – Programmes for professionals and executives
Available at: **http://www.steveprestonthecareercatalyst. com/career-coaching**

Portfolio Career Masterclass *– How to Work for Passion, Pleasure & Profit!*
Available at: **http://www.steveprestonthecareercatalyst. com/portfolio-careers/**

Audio book 2 MP3/CD set *– How Colourful is your umbrella*
Create a working life where you will enjoy Mondays as much as Fridays!
Available at: **http://www.steveprestonthecareercatalyst. com/product/colourful-umbrella-create-working-life-youll-enjoy-mondays-much-fridays/**

Career Change

Innovative and Inspirational Online Career Change & Transition Programme - *Navigate Your Way To A Brighter Future* – 6 steps to transform your career and life

> **SPECIAL READER OFFER:**
> Save £50 using code PC50-1-4

Available at: http://www.steveprestonthecareercatalyst. com/breakthrough-online-career-change-transition-programme/

Breakthrough Career Coaching with Steve – Programmes for professionals and executives
Available at: http://www.steveprestonthecareercatalyst. com/career-coaching

Career Values & Needs Exercise Tool

> **SPECIAL READER OFFER:**
> Save £10 using code CVN10

Available at: http://www.steveprestonthecareercatalyst. com/product/career-values-and-needs-exercise

Audio book 4 MP3/CD set – *I Want A Career Change* – 6 steps to navigate the way to a brighter future
Available at : http://www.steveprestonthecareercatalyst. com/product/i-want-a-career-change-4-mp3-set/

Book – *Winning Through Career Change* – Six steps to navigate your way to a brighter future *(Kindle version only)*
Available at: http://www.steveprestonthecareercatalyst. com/winning-through-career-change/

Redundancy

Book – *Winning Through Redundancy* – Six steps to navigate your way to a brighter future *(Kindle and paperback)* Available at: **http://www.steveprestonthecareercatalyst. com/about-steve-preston-the-career-catalyst/winning-through-redundancy/**

In addition, Steve has a toolkit of career change resources. These tools are to help you work towards achieving a successful career change, regardless of your situation. You can download this toolkit of resources by registering at: **http://www.steveprestonthecareercatalyst.com**

ABOUT

Steve Preston

Recognised as 'The Career Catalyst'®, Steve has transformed the lives and careers of thousands of people from many business sectors and walks of life. An internationally acclaimed author, speaker and leading career coach, Steve is passionate about helping unlock and fulfil people's potential. He especially enjoys helping people change their working lifestyle and develop portfolio careers to work for *Passion, Pleasure* and *Profit*!

Steve thrives on sharing his knowledge and experience to challenge your thinking about the world of work and what work you can do. He inspires people to follow your passions, do work you love and lead a fulfilling life. Steve runs breakthrough career development coaching programmes for professionals and executives and periodically unique Portfolio Career Masterclasses. He also has developed a highly acclaimed innovative online career change & transition programme and a wide range of inspirational career and personal development books and audio books.

Steve is a prolific writer, having written numerous articles for blogs, trade journals, career and personal development websites in the UK, US, Australia, New Zealand and LinkedIn Pulse. Steve is also a keynote motivational speaker at high profile career events, conferences and professional associations and has been featured around the globe in media interviews, radio shows and podcasts.

A key part of Steve's portfolio career is also as MD and Owner of specialist consultancy, SMP Solutions (Career & People Development) Ltd, providing quality outplacement, career transition and people development programmes, especially for organisations undergoing key change.

How to book or connect with Steve

If you would like to engage Steve to speak at your event, coach or mentor you, sign up for his blogs, learn more about his many products and services or just become part of his online communities, please contact or follow him by any of the following means...

Email: **steve@steveprestonthecareercatalyst.com**

Website: **www.steveprestonthecareercatalyst.com**

Facebook:
https://www.facebook.com/TheCareerCatalyst

Twitter:
https://twitter.com/stevempreston

LinkedIn:
http://www.linkedin.com/in/steveprestonsmpsolutions

SMP Solutions (Career & People Development) Ltd:
www.smp-solutions.co.uk

YouTube Channel:
https://www.youtube.com/channel/UCj0dyVi9gborbV0fLSZ7iow?view_as=public

18100621R00134

Printed in Great Britain
by Amazon